MARGARET FELICE

2019

A BOOK OF
GRACE-FILLED
DAYS

LOYOLAPRESS.
A JESUIT MINISTRY

Chicago

LOYOLA PRESS.
A JESUIT MINISTRY

3441 N. Ashland Avenue
Chicago, Illinois 60657
(800) 621-1008
www.loyolapress.com

Cover and interior design by Kathy Kikkert.

ISBN: 978-0-8294-4608-1
Library of Congress Control Number: 2018940519

Printed in the United States of America.
18 19 20 21 22 23 24 25 26 27 Bang 10 9 8 7 6 5 4 3 2 1

INTRODUCTION

What are you looking for?

This question has the power to shape our days. Our busy world is crammed full of excitement, stimulation, and countless distractions. You may have to go in search of peace, beauty, and grace to help you find the answer. But Jesus himself tells us, "Seek, and ye shall find."

My mother knows how to do this. One of the sounds I associate with my childhood is the rapid, mechanical click that a disposable camera made as the user advanced the film. My mother (who recently—finally—learned to use the camera on her phone) spent years with a disposable camera in her purse, ready to document whatever delighted her.

She'd snap photos of crocuses in bloom, tomatoes from the garden lined up to ripen on the windowsill, and the car odometer turning over to a nice, round number. In a twentieth-century world devoid of social media sharing, she went looking for special things to savor, and she found them. And I'd know something was making her smile when I heard that mechanical click.

My father, on the other hand, preferred a "real" camera with film, though he, too, has now figured out cell phone photography. As an oldest child, I was the subject of countless photos, each shutter click a reminder that there was someone looking at me with great love. Those two sounds of capturing memories have in turn been captured in my heart, symbols of love from my earliest days.

Are you ready to go looking for delight? Each day is full of grace, whether we perceive it or not. Sometimes the Holy Spirit startles us into seeing, but more often grace becomes apparent in simple, subtle moments. It is my hope that these passages and the daily Scripture will help you become more aware of the grace that flows throughout your day. For when we are looking for such moments, we are more likely to find them. And when we see that those moments are ongoing, that they string into days and months and years, we can pray ever more confidently with the words of St. Ignatius of Loyola: *Give me only your love and your grace, that is enough for me.*

DECEMBER 2

• FIRST SUNDAY OF ADVENT •

*The days are coming, says the LORD, when I will fulfill the
promise I made to the house of Israel and Judah.*
—JEREMIAH 33:14

The days are coming. Advent reminds us of the
tension between living in expectation and
recognizing the blessedness of the here and now.
When the world feels chaotic and violent, we look
forward to God's reign of peace. Can we also hold in
our hearts gratitude for all that we have now?

Jeremiah 33:14–16
Psalm 25:4–5,8–9,10,14 (1b)
1 Thessalonians 3:12–4:2
Luke 21:25–28,34–36

Monday

DECEMBER 3

• ST. FRANCIS XAVIER, PRIEST •

All nations shall stream toward it;
many peoples shall come and say:
"Come, let us climb the LORD's mountain,
to the house of the God of Jacob,
That he may instruct us in his ways,
and we may walk in his paths."
For from Zion shall go forth instruction,
and the word of the LORD from Jerusalem.
—ISAIAH 2:2–3

What mountains must I climb to reach the house of God?
What must I sacrifice? St. Francis Xavier had to shed his
vanity and pride, leaving behind a promising teaching
career in Paris for a life of celibacy, poverty, and service.
By doing this and following his friend Ignatius into
ministry and evangelization, he let his light shine even
brighter. What do you need to leave behind to follow the
path of God?

Isaiah 2:1–5
Psalm 122:1–2,3–4b,4cd–5,6–7,8–9
Matthew 8:5–11

⇒ 2 ⇐

Tuesday

DECEMBER 4

• ST. JOHN DAMASCENE, PRIEST AND DOCTOR OF THE CHURCH •

Jesus rejoiced in the Holy Spirit and said, "I give you praise,
Father, Lord of heaven and earth, for although you have
hidden these things from the wise and the learned you have
revealed them to the childlike. Yes, Father, such has been your
gracious will."
—LUKE 10:21

Lord, I pray today that I may clear away the
presuppositions and judgments that prevent me from
knowing your will. May I be as open as a child as I
seek to know you better.

Isaiah 11:1–10
Psalm 72:1–2,7–8,12–13,17
Luke 10:21–24

DECEMBER 5

On this mountain the LORD of hosts
will provide for all peoples
A feast of rich food and choice wines,
juicy, rich food and pure, choice wines.
—ISAIAH 25:6

The God of abundance and delight wants to lavish
good things on us. The image of juicy, rich food and
pure, choice wines in today's Scripture reading may
attract us and fill us with longing. But are we
similarly attracted to the life of generosity and virtue
to which we are called? Can we trust that it will lead
us to even greater satisfaction?

Isaiah 25:6–10a
Psalm 23:1–3a,3b–4,5,6
Matthew 15:29–37

It is better to take refuge in the LORD
than to trust in man.
—PSALM 118:8

For many years, I resisted trusting people because I immaturely confused cynicism with wisdom. As I grew to know myself better, I chose to trust because I realized that betrayal or disappointment could not change my innate sense of self and that the rewards of trusting were always more satisfying than my futile attempts at self-protection. God was my foundation, and that set me free.

Isaiah 26:1–6
Psalm 118:1 and
8–9,19–21,25–27a
Matthew 7:21,24–27

DECEMBER 7

• ST. AMBROSE, BISHOP AND DOCTOR OF THE CHURCH •

Wait for the LORD with courage;
be stouthearted, and wait for the LORD.
—PSALM 27:14

Fourth-century Milan, like much of the newly Christian
world, was divided by theological controversy over the
nature of Jesus. When the prefect of the city,
St. Ambrose, told the battling factions to knock it off,
legend has it that a voice from the back of the room
shouted, "Ambrose for bishop!" and a few days later he
was baptized and ordained. He couldn't have known, as
he studied law and worked in civil government, that he
was preparing to lead the Church. Or that one day he
would be recognized as a saint. During this season of
preparation, we acknowledge that often our preparations
make us ready for unforeseen acts of service.

Isaiah 29:17–24
Psalm 27:1,4,13–14
Matthew 9:27–31

DECEMBER 8

• THE IMMACULATE CONCEPTION OF THE BLESSED VIRGIN MARY
(PATRONAL FEASTDAY OF THE UNITED STATES OF AMERICA) •

*And coming to her, he said, "Hail, full of grace! The Lord
is with you."*
—LUKE 1:28

The Lord is with you. Be attentive to that message
today. Be reminded that we all have been created full
of grace and dignity.

Genesis 3:9–15,20
Psalm 98:1,2–3ab,3cd–4
Ephesians 1:3–6,11–12
Luke 1:26–38

I am confident of this, that the one who began a good work in you will continue to complete it until the day of Christ Jesus.
—PHILIPPIANS 1:6

As an educator, I see only a snapshot of a person's life: a few hours a day for a year or two. I don't always see what my students become, but I trust that their growth continues. I don't need to do it all, but I can be confident that the Lord will continue to complete his good work.

Baruch 5:1–9
Psalm 126:1–2,2–3,4–5,6 (3)
Philippians 1:4–6,8–11
Luke 3:1–6

DECEMBER 10

Say to those whose hearts are frightened:
Be strong, fear not!
—ISAIAH 35:4A

I live in New England, where the weather turns quite
cold in December. I huddle beneath warm layers as I
rush through the holiday madness. In the process, I
can easily miss the people near me who might need
a word of comfort or those who, instead of words,
need a listening ear and a warm heart. If you find
yourself in a similar situation, take some time today
to pause and notice those around you who may need
your presence.

Isaiah 35:1–10
Psalm 85:9ab and
10,11–12,13–14
Luke 5:17–26

Sing to the LORD a new song;
sing to the LORD, all you lands.
—PSALM 96:1

I have been involved in music ministry for decades, and around this time of year it feels like there are no new songs. We cycle through the "greatest hits" of seasonal hymnody so frequently that I am tempted to let my mind wander when making music. Yet this repetition is a grace of the season. We come back to these themes over and over, making them new with the changes in our lives from the previous year. Each song is made new not with our lips but with our hearts.

Isaiah 40:1–11
Psalm 96:1–2,3 and
10ac,11–12,13
Matthew 18:12–14

DECEMBER 12

• OUR LADY OF GUADALUPE •

Many nations shall join themselves to the LORD on that day,
and they shall be his people, and he will dwell among you,
and you shall know that the LORD of hosts has sent
me to you.
—ZECHARIAH 2:15

La Virgen de Guadalupe appeared in
sixteenth-century Mexico as a woman of mixed
indigenous and European descent to an indigenous
peasant. This would have been scandalous to many
Catholics of the time who were convinced of
European superiority. But her appearance reminds us
that we can never be surprised by God's messengers.
The word goes out to all nations, each one created
and loved by God.

Zechariah 2:14–17 or
Revelation 11:19a,12:1–6a,10ab
Judith 13:18bcde,19
Luke 1:26–38 or 1:39–47

DECEMBER 13

• ST. LUCY, VIRGIN AND MARTYR •

I will extol you, O my God and King,
and I will bless your name forever and ever.
—PSALM 145:1

St. Lucy, whose name means "light" in Latin, was
known for glowing with her love of God. Today,
she's celebrated around the world with processions
of candles, bringing light to this dark Advent season.
St. Lucy, you whose light illuminates the gospel and
leads hearts to Christ, pray that we might also be
lights revealing God's goodness and fidelity.

Isaiah 41:13–20
Psalm 145:1 and
9,10–11,12–13ab
Matthew 11:11–15

DECEMBER 14

• ST. JOHN OF THE CROSS, PRIEST AND DOCTOR OF THE CHURCH •

Thus says the LORD, your redeemer,
the Holy One of Israel:
I, the LORD, your God,
teach you what is for your good,
and lead you on the way you should go.
—ISAIAH 48:17

God's commands are not life-squelching but life-giving. Living out the law of love has required me to resist selfishness, impulsivity, and superiority. This obedience to God's commands has also deepened relationships in my life and helped me engage patiently and positively with those I encounter. In what ways has obedience enriched your life?

Isaiah 48:17–19
Psalm 1:1–2,3,4 and 6
Matthew 11:16–19

DECEMBER 15

Lord, make us turn to you;
let us see your face and we shall be saved.
—PSALM 80:4

Faith is like a dance: we ask our partner to turn
toward us, and we also must turn in order to meet.
When I ask God to speak, I pray for the grace to
listen. When I ask God to teach me, I pray for the
grace to learn.

Sirach 48:1–4,9–11
Psalm 80:2ac and
3b,15–16,18–19
Matthew 17:9a,10–13

DECEMBER 16

• THIRD SUNDAY OF ADVENT •

The crowds asked John the Baptist, "What should we do?" He said to them in reply, "Whoever has two cloaks should share with the person who has none. And whoever has food should do likewise."

—LUKE 3:10–11

The pre-Christmas messages of indulgence and spending are coming full force. In the midst of this season, take a breath and remember that our vocation is not to wealth. Our vocation is to discipleship. As Blessed Archbishop Óscar Romero once said, "Aspire not to have more but to be more."

Zephaniah 3:14–18a
Isaiah 12:2–3,4,5–6 (6)
Philippians 4:4–7
Luke 3:10–18

DECEMBER 17

Justice shall flower in his days,
and profound peace, till the moon be no more.
—PSALM 72:7

Tonight the Church begins praying the
O Antiphons, a series of verses that are sung or
chanted proclaiming the coming of our Savior. The
antiphons call Jesus by many different titles:
Wisdom, Adonai, Root of Jesse, Key of David,
Morning Star, King of Nations, Emmanuel. All these
titles help us voice our desire for Jesus to come into
our hearts and to the world with flourishing justice
and fullness of peace.

Genesis 49:2,8–10
Psalm 72:1–2,3–4ab,7–8,17
Matthew 1:1–17

DECEMBER 18

Behold, the days are coming, says the LORD,
when I will raise up a righteous shoot to David;
As king he shall reign and govern wisely,
he shall do what is just and right in the land.
—JEREMIAH 23:5

We don't need to be monarchs to reign and govern
wisely. No matter what form our power takes, any
time we use our authority with care, we are more
like Christ.

Jeremiah 23:5–8
Psalm 72:1–2,12–13,18–19
Matthew 1:18–25

DECEMBER 19

*Zechariah was troubled by what he saw, and fear
came upon him.*
—LUKE 1:12

If the Scripture is any indication, angels can be
pretty scary. In Numbers 22, an angel appears with a
sword, and in 2 Samuel 24, an angel prepares to
wipe out Jerusalem. Even when they come with
messages rather than weapons, they may give us
pause. And why shouldn't they? They bring the
awesome word of God. Even when their messages
are answers to our prayers, we still may tremble in
the face of God's messengers.

Judges 13:2–7,24–25a
Psalm 71:3–4a,5–6ab,16–17
Luke 1:5–25

Thursday

DECEMBER 20

*Who can ascend the mountain of the LORD?
or who may stand in his holy place?
He whose hands are sinless, whose heart is clean,
who desires not what is vain.*
—PSALM 24:3–4

Preparation may be on your mind as Christmas
approaches. Gifts, chores, baking, and travel all
remind us of this theme. As we prepare our homes
and our menus, are we also preparing our hearts to
encounter Christ, however we may meet him? Pause
today and look for our ever-present Savior
and friend.

Isaiah 7:10–14
Psalm 24:1–2,3–4ab,5–6
Luke 1:26–38

Hark! my lover—here he comes
springing across the mountains,
leaping across the hills.
—SONG OF SONGS 2:8

Before we married, my husband and I were in a
long-distance relationship for four years. One silver
lining to those grueling years of separation was that
we were always excited to see each other. Even now
our eyes light up when we see each other after being
apart. I believe this is how God looks at each of us:
full of energy, love, and delight.

Song of Songs 2:8–14 or
Zephaniah 3:14–18a
Psalm 33:2–3,11–12,20–21
Luke 1:39–45

DECEMBER 22

He has shown the strength of his arm,
and has scattered the proud in their conceit.
He has cast down the mighty from their thrones
and has lifted up the lowly.
—LUKE 1:51–52

Stay awake and be ready. We may be tempted to
imagine that our readiness consists in being well
stocked and protected, sealed in our bunkers. But the
readiness to which we are called is the readiness of a
lowly and open heart that Mary models. We prepare
ourselves not by having more but by having less. Do
not be beguiled by worldly strength and pride.

1 Samuel 1:24–28
1 Samuel 2:1,4–5,6–7,8abcd
Luke 1:46–56

DECEMBER 23

• FOURTH SUNDAY OF ADVENT •

"Blessed are you who believed that what was spoken to you by the Lord would be fulfilled."
—LUKE 1:45

Mary's radical trust leaves as strong an impression now as it did thousands of years ago. We, too, are blessed when we have faith in God's promises. I have felt called to work in the Church since I was quite young, but with a big, impulsive personality, I never quite fit the mold, at least in the eyes of others. At times I was discouraged from following my calling because people couldn't envision someone like me in ministry. Still, I have remained faithful to the call and the promise that it is what I am meant for, no matter what the world may think.

Micah 5:1–4a
Psalm 80:2–3,15–16,18–19 (4)
Hebrews 10:5–10
Luke 1:39–45

Monday

DECEMBER 24

*Zechariah his father, filled with the Holy Spirit,
prophesied, saying:
"Blessed be the Lord, the God of Israel;
for he had come to his people and set them free."*
—LUKE 1:67–68

God never stops coming to us. No matter how
receptive we are, God is always ready with the
graces that will free us. For many, Christmas can be a
difficult season in which family tensions or other
hardships bubble up. If there is something holding
you back from the spirit of Christmas, know that
God is there, ready to free you of that stress,
sadness, or worry.

2 Samuel 7:1–5,8b–12,14a,16
Psalm 89:2–3,4–5,27 and 29
Luke 1:67–79

Tuesday

DECEMBER 25

• THE NATIVITY OF THE LORD (CHRISTMAS) •

How beautiful upon the mountains
are the feet of him who brings glad tidings,
announcing peace, bearing good news,
announcing salvation, and saying to Zion,
"Your God is King!"
—ISAIAH 52:7

If you have been bombarded with seasonal
advertising and promotions, there may still be a
message you are longing to hear. Take a quiet
moment to observe what Christ is saying to
you today.

VIGIL:
Isaiah 62:1–5
Psalm 89:4–5,16–17,27,29 (2a)
Acts 13:16–17,22–25
Matthew 1:1–25 or 1:18–25

NIGHT:
Isaiah 9:1–6
Psalm 96:1–2,2–3,11–12,13
Titus 2:11–14
Luke 2:1–14

DAWN:
Isaiah 62:11–12
Psalm 97:1,6,11–12
Titus 3:4–7
Luke 2:15–20

DAY:
Isaiah 52:7–10
Psalm 98:1,2–3,3–4,5–6 (3c)
Hebrews 1:1–6
John 1:1–18 or 1:1–5,9–14

DECEMBER 26

But they cried out in a loud voice, covered their ears, and rushed upon him together.
—ACTS 7:57

In a speech to the Sanhedrin, St. Stephen recounts the history of God at work in the people of Israel and how the Israelites often turned their backs on God. He admonishes his audience, calling them "stubborn people" who resist the Holy Spirit. In response, the crowd cover their ears, unwilling to hear his words, and stones him. I'm ashamed to admit how much I relate to St. Stephen's persecutors. There have been times I've longed to cover my ears to keep out ideas I didn't want to hear. When confronted with words that challenge me, I must keep my ears open and consider if there is something I am meant to learn.

Acts 6:8–10,7:54–59
Psalm 31:3cd–4,6 and 8ab,16bc and 17
Matthew 10:17–22

DECEMBER 27

• ST. JOHN, APOSTLE AND EVANGELIST •

We are writing this so that our joy may be complete.
—1 JOHN 1:4

St. John the Evangelist shared the truth of Christ so that more would know it. I strive for a joyful faith that I can't help but share with others, that inspires me to include everyone.

1 John 1:1–4
Psalm 97:1–2,5–6,11–12
John 20:1a,2–8

When Herod realized that he had been deceived by the magi,
he became furious. He ordered the massacre of all the boys in
Bethlehem and its vicinity two years old and under, in
accordance with the time he had ascertained from the magi.
—MATTHEW 2:16

The forces of darkness are violent and
overwhelming. How astonishing that God came into
the world in the form of a vulnerable baby. It takes
great trust to be confident that weakness can be
strength and that light can drive out darkness. May
we pray for this confidence today.

1 John 1:5–2:2
Psalm 124:2–3,4–5,7b–8
Matthew 2:13–18

Beloved: The way we may be sure that we know Jesus is to keep his commandments.

—1 JOHN 2:3

Our actions reveal our values. We can't claim faith and then ignore the instruction to love our neighbor. I do my best to live the commandment of love every day, showing affection to my friends and family and care for my students. Yet I encounter far more people than that every day and know that I need to expand the circle of love beyond the bounds of my tribe, just as Jesus did.

1 John 2:3–11
Psalm 96:1–2a, 2b–3,5b–6
Luke 2:22–35

DECEMBER 30

• THE HOLY FAMILY OF JESUS, MARY, AND JOSEPH •

And Jesus advanced in wisdom and age and favor before
God and man.
—LUKE 2:52

We know so little about Jesus' life growing up. In his
book *Leaping*, Brian Doyle writes, "If we remember
only the legend of this man, and not the skinny,
intense, confusing man himself, we do him disservice
and disrespect, for he was once one of us, which is
to say he is us." Although the daily details may not
be filled in, we do know the fullness of the man who
came to be, and we set aside a Sunday to remember
that he, too, was part of a family, with all the
conflict and joy that entails.

1 Samuel 1:20–22,24–28 or
Sirach 3:2–6,12–14
Psalm 84:2–3,5–6,9–10
1 John 3:1–2,21–24 or
Colossians 3:12–21 or 3:12–17
Luke 2:41–52

In the beginning was the Word,
and the Word was with God,
and the Word was God.
—JOHN 1:1

Beginnings and endings may be on your mind today.
We say goodbye to what came before and embark
on something new, with God always a part of every
beginning and end. We can enter into the unknown
with hope and courage because we know that the
Word is in all times and places. And we meet God
anew with each new endeavor. As T. S. Eliot writes
in "Little Gidding," "And the end of all our exploring
/ will be to arrive where we started / and know the
place for the first time."

1 John 2:18–21
Psalm 96:1–2,11–12,13
John 1:1–18

Tuesday

JANUARY 1

• SOLEMNITY OF MARY, THE HOLY MOTHER OF GOD •

*And Mary kept all these things, reflecting on them
in her heart.*
—LUKE 2:19

Whether your heart is filled with excitement or
anxiety as the new year dawns, let it expand in love.

Numbers 6:22–27
Psalm 67:2–3,5,6,8 (2a)
Galatians 4:4–7
Luke 2:16–21

JANUARY 2

• SS. BASIL THE GREAT AND GREGORY NAZIANZEN, BISHOPS AND DOCTORS
OF THE CHURCH •

The LORD has made his salvation known:
in the sight of the nations he has revealed his justice.
—PSALM 98:2

In these early days of the year, are there things God
is trying to make known to you? If you looked past
your routine, could you see more clearly how God is
leading you?

1 John 2:22–28
Psalm 98:1,2–3ab,3cd–4
John 1:19–28

Thursday

JANUARY 3

• THE MOST HOLY NAME OF JESUS •

"Now I have seen and testified that he is the Son of God."
—JOHN 1:34

I am often too casual in invoking Jesus' Holy Name,
and the language I use to discuss others doesn't
always respect their dignity. When my words do not
reflect what I wish were in my heart, I need to
repent and recommit to speech that gives life and
love to all. Words matter.

1 John 2:29—3:6
Psalm 98:1,3cd–4,5–6
John 1:29–34

Friday

JANUARY 4

• ST. ELIZABETH ANN SETON, RELIGIOUS •

Children, let no one deceive you. The person who acts in
righteousness is righteous, just as he is righteous.
—1 JOHN 3:7

Do your actions demonstrate that you are a friend of
God? Do you live with a humility that lets you be
honest about both your failings and your gifts? Being
honest about our struggles and our strengths helps us
live with humble confidence, and this confidence
always helps us respect others.

1 John 3:7–10
Psalm 98:1,7–8,9
John 1:35–42

JANUARY 5

• ST. JOHN NEUMANN, BISHOP •

Jesus decided to go to Galilee, and he found Philip. And Jesus said to him, "Follow me."
—JOHN 1:43

We follow Jesus through drudgery and exhaustion, through trials and sorrow, through excitement and fervor, through labor, through rest. St. John Neumann advised, "As Christ has His work, we too have ours; as He rejoiced to do His work, we must rejoice in ours also." John Neumann is best known for transforming the diocese of Philadelphia in the mid-1800s, as the number of parishes grew and the Catholic school system was developing. Before this time, as an immigrant priest and later a naturalized citizen, he had lonely and grueling placements in other parts of the eastern United States. We can emulate the prayer, faith, and discipline he must have had to stay joyful in a life of such service.

1 John 3:11–21
Psalm 100:1b–2,3,4,5
John 1:43–51

Sunday

JANUARY 6

• THE EPIPHANY OF THE LORD •

*Nations shall walk by your light,
and kings by your shining radiance.*
—ISAIAH 60:3

When the glory of the Lord is revealed, its light
illuminates the people. May we not only see the
light but reflect it so that others may come to know
God's glory.

Isaiah 60:1–6
Psalm 72:1–2,7–8,10–11,12–13
Ephesians 3:2–3a,5–6
Matthew 2:1–12

JANUARY 7

• ST. RAYMOND OF PENYAFORT, PRIEST •

From that time on, Jesus began to preach and say, "Repent,
for the Kingdom of heaven is at hand."
—MATTHEW 4:17

Repentance is not a onetime event. It is a constant
reorienting of our hearts so that we are heading in
the right direction: toward Christ.

1 John 3:22–4:6
Psalm 2:7bc–8,10–12a
Matthew 4:12–17,23–25

JANUARY 8

By now it was already late and his disciples approached him and said, "This is a deserted place and it is already very late. Dismiss them so that they can go to the surrounding farms and villages and buy themselves something to eat." He said to them in reply, "Give them some food yourselves."
—MARK 6:35–37

"Someone should really do something about that." Do you ever find yourself saying that? At times, the work to be done exceeds our purview or our expertise. But sometimes the task I imagine for someone else is an act of charity that I myself ought to do.

1 John 4:7–10
Psalm 72:1–2,3–4,7–8
Mark 6:34–44

JANUARY 9

No one has ever seen God. Yet, if we love one another, God remains in us, and his love is brought to perfection in us.
—1 JOHN 4:12

To see God—to know God—we must love. How incredible is it that God's boundless love can be brought to perfection in the bonds we have with one another! The Jesuit philosopher Pierre Teilhard de Chardin, SJ, seems to understand this when he writes, "Someday, after mastering the winds, the waves, the tides and gravity, we shall harness for God the energies of love, and then, for a second time in the history of the world, man will have discovered fire."

1 John 4:11–18
Psalm 72:1–2,10,12–13
Mark 6:45–52

May his name be blessed forever;
as long as the sun his name shall remain.
In him shall all the tribes of the earth be blessed;
all the nations shall proclaim his happiness.
—PSALM 72:17

After more than a decade of studying and teaching
Church history, I am convinced that the continued
existence of the Church is a sign that God is with us.
Our foibles and sins would have wrecked it beyond
salvaging long ago if not for the grace of the One
whose name shall remain as long as the sun.

1 John 4:19–5:4
Psalm 72:1–2,14 and 15bc,17
Luke 4:14–22a

It happened that there was a man full of leprosy in one of the towns where Jesus was; and when he saw Jesus, he fell prostrate, pleaded with him, and said, "Lord, if you wish, you can make me clean."
—LUKE 5:12

In desperate times, I have prayed desperate prayers for healing and change. At times, chronic illness put me in ferocious physical pain, and, at its worst, drew from me a raw and fierce prayer to end my suffering, cutting through the detachment I often bring to prayer. Even though these prayers were not answered with immediate relief, I benefited from opening myself fully to Jesus and drawing closer to him in my need.

1 John 5:5–13
Psalm 147:12–13,14–15,19–20
Luke 5:12–16

JANUARY 12

Children, be on your guard against idols.
—1 JOHN 5:21

Two of the idols that most tempt me are security and
pride. I want my life to be safe and consistent. I fear
embarrassing myself or revealing that there are
things I don't know. These idols hold me back,
blocking my path as I walk the way of discipleship.
When I become aware of what stands in the way of
growth, I try to look beyond those idols toward the
ultimate goals that hold more promise for me than
false gods. This vision motivates me to push my
idols to the side and risk the vulnerability that leads
to deeper freedom.

1 John 5:14–21
Psalm 149:1–2,3–4,5 and 6a and 9b
John 3:22–30

JANUARY 13

• THE BAPTISM OF THE LORD •

Go up onto a high mountain,
Zion, herald of glad tidings;
cry out at the top of your voice,
Jerusalem, herald of good news!
Fear not to cry out
and say to the cities of Judah:
Here is your God!
—ISAIAH 40:9

Baptism makes us part of the prophetic ministry of the Church and of Christ. Every time we proclaim the Lord with our mouths or our lives, we continue Jesus' ministry.

Isaiah 40:1–5,9–11 or 42:1–4,6–7
Psalm 104:1b–2,3–4,24–25,27–28,29–30 (1)
Titus 2:11–14,3:4–7 or Acts 10:34–38
Luke 3:15–16,21–22

*Then he called them. So they left their father Zebedee in the
boat along with the hired men and followed him.*
—MARK 1:20

We often hear the saying, "What are you waiting for,
an engraved invitation?" Although it's rarely
engraved, we are constantly invited to grow closer
to Jesus. Are there people in your life who have
helped you hear that call? And are there people in
your life in need of that call whom you could help
recognize this invitation to God's heart?

Hebrews 1:1–6
Psalm 97:1 and 2b,6 and 7c,9
Mark 1:14–20

JANUARY 15

He cried out, "What have you to do with us, Jesus of Nazareth? Have you come to destroy us? I know who you are—the Holy One of God!"
—MARK 1:24

In today's reading, a man with an unclean spirit speaks the truth: Jesus is the Holy One of God. Yet this spirit sees danger in Jesus' presence. There is danger in following Jesus: you may be asked to change your life or to make sacrifices. But we know his power to drive out the darkness, and we know that following him toward the light is worth any sacrifice.

Hebrews 2:5–12
Psalm 8:2ab and 5,6–7,8–9
Mark 1:21–28

JANUARY 16

He remembers forever his covenant.
—PSALM 105:8

God made an everlasting covenant, agreeing to accompany humanity for all time. What an astonishing gift! Despite our failings, the Lord remembers this promise, loving us and desiring to be with us. Let this be a comfort in times of anxiety or sadness. God will never leave our side.

Hebrews 2:14–18
Psalm 105:1–2,3–4,6–7,8–9
Mark 1:29–39

Thursday

JANUARY 17

• ST. ANTHONY, ABBOT •

*Take care, brothers and sisters, that none of you may have an
evil and unfaithful heart, so as to forsake the living God.*
—HEBREWS 3:12

Tending to our own hearts is an essential component
of prayer. An open heart is able to respond in love to
others. A faithful heart remembers that fidelity to
God's law is preferable to all of the world's
temptations. If the busyness of life threatens to
harden your heart, seek those moments of quiet and
wonder to soften it again.

Hebrews 3:7–14
Psalm 95:6–7c,8–9,10–11
Mark 1:40–45

⇒ 47 ⇐

Friday

JANUARY 18

What we have heard and know,
and what our fathers have declared to us,
we will declare to the generation to come
The glorious deeds of the LORD and his strength.
—PSALM 78:3–4

Do the stories you tell give glory to God? Consider the stories you cherished from your own childhood. Maybe you loved to hear the story of how your parents met, or when a sibling was born, or when your grandparents emigrated to a new country. As children, we long to hear of heroism and happiness, but in adulthood, we may be tempted to dwell on frustrations and hardships. It is the stories of everyday miracles that witness to God's goodness. What are the stories you will pass on to generations to come?

Hebrews 4:1–5,11
Psalm 78:3 and 4bc,6c–7,8
Mark 2:1–12

The word of God is living and effective, sharper than any two-edged sword, penetrating even between soul and spirit, joints and marrow, and able to discern reflections and thoughts of the heart.
—HEBREWS 4:12

The mere fact that God's word has been passed down through the ages is testament to its power. God has spoken in Scripture, in inspired writings of holy people, and in whispers in our own hearts. The words of Jesus particularly penetrate my spirit, as they come from a living God who exhibited such perfect integrity and love while on earth. Which of God's words penetrate your soul today?

Hebrews 4:12–16
Psalm 19:8,9,10,15
Mark 2:13–17

JANUARY 20

• SECOND SUNDAY IN ORDINARY TIME •

*Jesus did this as the beginning of his signs at Cana in Galilee,
and so revealed his glory, and his disciples began to
believe in him.*
—JOHN 2:11

As a child, I used to pore over a beloved version of
Jesus' miracle at Cana in a book called *The Feast that
Almost Flopped*. My mother read it to me often. We
giggled over the silly title and reveled over how
Jesus gave such a miraculous gift to the host of this
feast. What better introduction to the gratuitous
generosity of Jesus' signs and wonders than laughing
and learning in the arms of someone who loved me?

Isaiah 62:1–5
Psalm 96:1–2,2–3,7–8,9–10 (3)
1 Corinthians 12:4–11
John 2:1–11

JANUARY 21

• ST. AGNES, VIRGIN AND MARTYR •

*The disciples of John and of the Pharisees were accustomed to
fast. People came to Jesus and objected,
"Why do the disciples of John and the disciples of the
Pharisees fast, but your disciples do not fast?"*
—MARK 2:18

Jesus disrupted the customs of how religious people
should act. Because of that, many people complained
and objected. The Pharisees were accustomed to
fasting, and in today's reading from Mark, they react
poorly to the lack of fasting among Jesus' disciples.
How is Jesus calling you to break your routine in
order to better follow him? Listen for ways in which
God is calling you to newness, even if the call is
disruptive.

Hebrews 5:1–10
Psalm 110:1,2,3,4
Mark 2:18–22

JANUARY 22

• DAY OF PRAYER FOR THE LEGAL PROTECTION OF UNBORN CHILDREN •

I will give thanks to the LORD with all my heart,
in the company and assembly of the just.
—PSALM 111:1

The communities in which we worship are truly
sacred, and we are fortunate when we find people
with whom we can jointly offer our praise. When I
read today's words of the psalmist, which specifically
mention giving thanks with others, I am reminded
that my faith is fulfilled in community.

Hebrews 6:10–20
Psalm 111:1–2,4–5,9 and 10c
Mark 2:23–28

⋺ 52 ⋲

JANUARY 23

They watched Jesus closely to see if he would cure him on the sabbath so that they might accuse him.
—MARK 3:2

The Pharisees in the synagogue aren't able to truly see Jesus because they are only looking for things to criticize. I have been guilty of this, unable to see because I'm so eager to find a slight or insult. Imagine if we approached each person with the same attitude we bring to Jesus, expecting virtue and love. May we all expect the best of those in our lives today.

Hebrews 7:1–3,15–17
Psalm 110:1,2,3,4
Mark 3:1–6

Here am I, Lord; I come to do your will.
—PSALM 40:8–9

Throughout Scripture, there are examples of people offering their lives to God with the words "Here I am." What courage it takes to simply show up in front of God and offer one's complete self. Not only do we risk being asked to do something we fear, but we also must have the confidence to believe that we have something to offer, that we can be of service, and that God desires to be close to us, just as we are. What humility and force of faith is carried in those simple words.

Hebrews 7:25—8:6
Psalm 40:7–8a,8b–9,10,17
Mark 3:7–12

Friday

JANUARY 25

• THE CONVERSION OF ST. PAUL THE APOSTLE •

Praise the LORD all you nations;
glorify him, all you peoples!
—PSALM 117:1

On the Feast of the Conversion of Paul, the readings
highlight the global nature of the Church, the roots
of which can be credited in part to Paul and his
missionary work. The role of the missionary has
changed so much since Paul's time, but one thing has
not changed: the task of every Christian to
"proclaim the Gospel to every creature"
(Mark 16:15). We do this when we observe the
psalmist's admonition to praise and glorify God.

Acts 22:3–16 or 9:1–22
Psalm 117:1bc,2
Mark 16:15–18

⇒ 55 ⇐

I am grateful to God, whom I worship with a clear conscience as my ancestors did, as I remember you constantly in my prayers, night and day.

—2 TIMOTHY 1:3

St. Paul writes elsewhere that we should "pray always. "Today's reading from his letter to Timothy reveals that he prays "constantly." This idea has always made me anxious. How could I possibly live up to such a goal? My prayer life is unregimented—I'm more inclined to moments of spontaneous communication with God than to intentional prayer practices. I try to be disciplined about cultivating prayer, finding quiet times and spaces to focus on God and others. I also try to identify the hidden prayer moments and to move in the world with a disposition that makes every action constant prayer. In what ways do you find yourself consciously or unconsciously praying?

2 Timothy 1:1–8 or Titus 1:1–5
Psalm 96:1–2a,2b–3,7–8a,10
Mark 3:20–21

JANUARY 27

• THIRD SUNDAY IN ORDINARY TIME •

*He said further: "Go, eat rich foods and drink sweet drinks,
and allot portions to those who had nothing prepared; for
today is holy to our LORD. Do not be saddened this day, for
rejoicing in the LORD must be your strength!"*
—NEHEMIAH 8:10

Joyfully sharing food with those we love has long
been part of our worship. Rejoicing with our loved
ones is an important and wonderful way to express
praise and gratitude, but it is not the end of our task.
We must "allot portions to those who had nothing
prepared," even if we think they have been
irresponsible, wasteful, or lazy. Simple sharing is part
of following the Lord.

Nehemiah 8:2–4a, 5–6,8–10
Psalm 19:8,9, 10,15
1 Corinthians 12:12–30 or
12:12–14,27
Luke 1:1–4; 4:14–21

Sing praise to the LORD with the harp,
with the harp and melodious song.
With trumpets and the sound of the horn
sing joyfully before the King, the LORD.
—PSALM 98:5–6

I direct a liturgical choir at a high school. Our
ensemble accepts any instrumentalists who want to
join, which leads to some unusual instrumental
combinations. Each instrumentalist adds to the rich
texture of our prayer and to the unique dimensions
of our sound. The varied timbres, plus the collection
of voices, make it more likely that each person in the
congregation will hear something that encourages
him or her to add their own voice in praise. It's
worth taking a chance on sounds that might be
messy or unrefined if the result is that more people
will be drawn into that joyful noise.

Hebrews 9:15,24–28
Psalm 98:1,2–3ab,3cd–4,5–6
Mark 3:22–30

JANUARY 29

And looking around at those seated in the circle he said, "Here are my mother and my brothers. For whoever does the will of God is my brother and sister and mother."

—MARK 3:34–35

In today's reading, Jesus calls the crowd seated around him "my mother and my brothers." It's hard to read this story without imagining that Mary and the apostles seeking him outside the crowd felt rebuffed. But imagine instead that you were in this crowd. Jesus looks up and sees you. He stays with you. He is truly present, not preoccupied with wherever else he could be, not looking for someone more important. There is radical acceptance in the fact that he remains with you and calls you his kin.

Hebrews 10:1–10
Psalm 40:2 and 4ab,7–8a,10,11
Mark 3:31–35

JANUARY 30

Jesus said to them, "Do you not understand this parable?
Then how will you understand any of the parables?"
—MARK 4:13

I can very easily become frustrated when I feel
misunderstood. I don't want to take the time to
explain, and I think, *This should be easy to understand!*
When Jesus shares the parable of the sower with a
large crowd, he accepts that some of the Twelve
don't understand and later goes over each type of
soil with them one more time. Here we see Jesus as
consummate teacher, reviewing the material until the
Twelve get it. He can help us till the soil of our
hearts so that we are truly ready to hear the word,
accept it, and bear fruit from it.

Hebrews 10:11–18
Psalm 110:1,2,3,4
Mark 4:1–20

Thursday

JANUARY 31

• ST. JOHN BOSCO, PRIEST •

We must consider how to rouse one another to love and good
works. We should not stay away from our assembly, as is the
custom of some, but encourage one another, and this all the
more as you see the day drawing near.
—HEBREWS 10:24–25

There is a certain subset of seekers who explain their
avoidance of organized religion by stating that they
find God in the woods. I can certainly see the
attraction of that: the aroma of pine needles, soft
moss underfoot, dappled sunshine, chirping birds.
Privately beholding God's creation is part of the
spiritual life, but this passage from Hebrews reminds
us that community is part of our spiritual discipline.
Community is what Jesus built during his time and
what his apostles encouraged in their age. It is
challenging, but it is also essential.

Hebrews 10:19–25
Psalm 24:1–2,3–4ab,5–6
Mark 4:21–25

FEBRUARY 1

You need endurance to do the will of God and receive what he has promised.
—HEBREWS 10:36

Jesus' simple admonition to love one another proves remarkably complicated when we try to put it into practice. Distraction, cynicism, temptation, and weariness can pull us away from the path. Anyone who attempts discipleship understands this statement from the author of Hebrews: "You need endurance to do the will of God." Knowing that the path can be grueling, we can be gentle with ourselves along the way. The more clearly we can see the incarnate love we follow, the more deeply we will be drawn along this remarkable pathway.

Hebrews 10:32–39
Psalm 37:3–4,5–6,23–24,39–40
Mark 4:26–34

FEBRUARY 2

*Because he himself was tested through what he suffered, he is
able to help those who are being tested.*
—HEBREWS 2:18

Jesus' compassion for humankind reached its
pinnacle in the Passion. God suffered, just as we do.
I have experienced very painful years because of
chronic illness and was tested by pain and frailty.
Jesus was indeed able to help me, and, in a way, he
already had. By his sacrifice long ago on the cross
and his ongoing gift of himself in the Eucharist, he
made plain that even suffering can be sanctified, that
we can be both blessed and broken.

Malachi 3:1–4
Psalm 24:7,8,9,10
Hebrews 2:14–18
Luke 2:22–40 or 2:22–32

FEBRUARY 3

• FOURTH SUNDAY IN ORDINARY TIME •

In you, O LORD, I take refuge;
let me never be put to shame.
—PSALM 71:1

Like most people, I don't enjoy feelings of shame.
This motivates me to avoid sin, since the knowledge
that I have hurt another person rightly makes me
ashamed. But because I am human, I also find myself
ashamed when I am embarrassed because of less
serious faults. When this prideful shame overwhelms
me, I remind myself of what matters to God:
generosity, love, and even humility—that very thing
that pride urges me to reject. I pray to be ashamed
only of neglecting these virtues and of failing to take
refuge in the God who promises abundant life.

Jeremiah 1:4–5,17–19
Psalm 71:1–2,3–4,5–6,15,17
1 Corinthians 12:31–13:13 or 13:4–13
Luke 4:21–30

FEBRUARY 4

Then they began to beg him to leave their district.
—MARK 5:17

Early in my career, I had to make a decision that I
suspected would lead me in a difficult direction. I put off
praying about it because I didn't want to face the
upheaval that the right choice would bring to my life. Of
course, as soon as I took the situation to prayer, God
confirmed my hunch that the harder path was the right
one. So, I can relate to the townsfolk who witnessed Jesus
driving the demons out of a possessed man and into a
herd of swine. Even though his work is holy, it creates
frightening disorder. Part of my struggle in prayer is to
remember that God's presence is always better than
stability and that listening to God's voice is always more
life-giving than whatever comfort I fear might be
shaken up.

Hebrews 11:32–40
Psalm 31:20,21,22,23,24
Mark 5:1–20

FEBRUARY 5

• ST. AGATHA, VIRGIN AND MARTYR •

*Since we are surrounded by so great a cloud of witnesses, let us rid
ourselves of every burden and sin that clings to us and persevere in
running the race that lies before us while keeping our eyes fixed on
Jesus, the leader and perfecter of faith.*
—HEBREWS 12:1–2

These early weeks of Ordinary Time take the Church
through much of Hebrews, in which great theological
truths are expressed in stirring, poetic language. Some of
its phrases, like "cloud of witnesses," are now part of the
common parlance of faith. What a blessing to have such
a rich artistic tradition, to have a cloud of witnesses that
includes creative geniuses. In moments when our own
expression fails, we turn to the great writers, painters,
composers, and builders of the past. We can rest our
prayers on their shoulders of faith.

Hebrews 12:1–4
Psalm 22:26b–27,28 and 30,31–32
Mark 5:21–43

FEBRUARY 6

• ST. PAUL MIKI AND COMPANIONS, MARTYRS •

Jesus said to them, "A prophet is not without honor except in his native place and among his own kin and in his own house."
—MARK 6:4

Today's reading finds Jesus returning to his hometown, where he teaches in the synagogue and cures a few sick people. In response, the townspeople are astonished and offended, wondering how this man they know as the son of a carpenter received such wisdom and performed such deeds. The people in Jesus' native place let their familiarity with him blind them to the wisdom of his teaching. How often do we fail to see the truth because of bias or presupposition? In prayer and in life, it is helpful to check our vision, to ask God for clarity so we don't miss the truth.

Hebrews 12:4–7,11–15
Psalm 103:1–2,13–14,17–18a
Mark 6:1–6

FEBRUARY 7

He instructed them to take nothing for the journey but a
walking stick—no food, no sack, no money in their belts.
They were, however, to wear sandals but not a second tunic.
—MARK 6:8–9

When I teach a unit on monasticism to high
schoolers, I reiterate to my students this simple
lifestyle model of not owning (or speaking or
consuming) more than is necessary. Jesus' guidance
to the Twelve before they set out encourages
reflection on what is truly necessary. Take nothing,
he says, but sandals and your walking stick because
you need those to get around. For our share in that
same mission, we must determine what our
necessities are, so that we don't lean too far toward
indulgence or austerity.

Hebrews 12:18–19,21–24
Psalm 48:2–3ab,3cd–4,9, 10–11
Mark 6:7–13

The LORD is my light and my salvation;
whom should I fear?
—PSALM 27:1

On my best days, I move confidently in the world,
secure in God's love and care, and I can proclaim
assuredly the words of Psalm 27. Most of the time,
though, I hold at least a sliver of anxiety or concern
about some issue or another. Those are the days
when I truly need the psalms. I can always return to
the same words that have sustained prayers for
generations, knowing that they can move my heart
closer toward the perfect faith we all seek.

Hebrews 13:1–8
Psalm 27:1,3,5,8b–9abc
Mark 6:14–29

*Do not neglect to do good and to share what you have; God is
pleased by sacrifices of that kind.*
—HEBREWS 13:16

My entry into the study of theology was Scripture. I
loved the complexity of exploring a sacred text:
hypothesizing about intended audiences, searching
for cross-references, and researching historical
context. The deeper we get into the study of our
faith, the more complex our history and literature
can seem, which is why I cherish such simple advice
as this from Hebrews. The Christian life is one of
goodness and generosity. The smallest kindnesses
are pleasing to God. That message makes my study
of faith simple and clear.

Hebrews 13:15–17,20–21
Psalm 23:1–3a,3b–4,5,6
Mark 6:30–34

FEBRUARY 10

• FIFTH SUNDAY IN ORDINARY TIME •

But by the grace of God I am what I am, and his grace to me
has not been ineffective.
—1 CORINTHIANS 15:10

Each of today's readings demonstrates that God calls
the unexpected and even the sinful. Isaiah, Paul, and
Peter all see their sins but follow the voice of God.
Paul states it clearly: God's grace works in him, an
unlikely servant. Every person has a part in
advancing God's reign, regardless of past mistakes or
flaws. May God's forgiveness and grace give us the
courage to say, like so many, "Here I am, send me."

Isaiah 6:1–2a,3–8
Psalm 138:1–2,2–3,4–5,7–8 (1c)
1 Corinthians 15:1–11 or 15:3–8,11
Luke 5:1–11

They scurried about the surrounding country and began to bring in the sick on mats to wherever they heard he was.
—MARK 6:55

The Lourdes Hymn, known to many as "Immaculate Mary," is a traditional French tune with Marian lyrics added for use during processions at Lourdes. I can picture crowds of pilgrims singing the simple refrain of "Ave, ave, ave Maria!" through long rituals in this holy place where a poor girl had a vision that changed her life and the lives of many others. One of many messages of Lourdes is that God's word often comes to the lowly and that the common people bring that word to life, just as they did in Jesus' time when the crowds followed him.

Genesis 1:1–19
Psalm 104:1–2a,5–6,10 and
12,24 and 35c
Mark 6:53–56

FEBRUARY 12

Such is the story of the heavens and the earth at their creation.
—GENESIS 2:4

The story of the creation of the world will be
proclaimed again later this year at the Easter Vigil.
On that night, we will hear this account while sitting
in the dark, remembering God's everlasting
goodness. We will await the ringing of the bells, the
singing of the *Gloria*, and the gift we are about to be
given in Christ's Death and Resurrection. Compared
with that dramatic night, a Tuesday in February feels
like an anticlimactic time to hear these words from
Genesis, but they remind me that God's magnificent
graciousness is as true in the mundane as it is in
the festive.

Genesis 1:20—2:4a
Psalm 8:4–5,6–7,8–9
Mark 7:1–13

Wednesday

FEBRUARY 13

Bless the LORD, O my soul!
—PSALM 104:1

What has most recently inspired you to bless the
Lord? What has so filled you with joy or wonder
that you couldn't help but exclaim your praise?
Those moments when our hearts shine with
gratitude are times of prayer.

Genesis 2:4b–9,15–17
Psalm 104:1–2a,27–28,29bc–30
Mark 7:14–23

⇒ 74 ⇐

FEBRUARY 14

• SS. CYRIL, MONK, AND METHODIUS, BISHOP •

The LORD God said: "It is not good for the man to be alone. I will make a suitable partner for him."
—GENESIS 2:18

In stressful times, we might envy Adam's situation: alone and peaceful in a quiet, beautiful garden. But this foundational myth testifies to the truth of human nature: we need companionship. The intimacy God extends to Adam, sealed by breathing life directly into the first man's mouth, is fundamental to who we are. Relationship completes us. What relationship can you nurture today?

Genesis 2:18–25
Psalm 128:1–2,3,4–5
Mark 7:24–30

FEBRUARY 15

*He took him off by himself away from the crowd. He put his
finger into the man's ears and, spitting, touched his tongue;
then he looked up to heaven and groaned, and said to him,
"Ephphatha!" (that is, "Be opened!")*
—MARK 7:33–34

If asked to envision Jesus, I picture a gleaming,
immaculate figure in white robes and soft focus who
gazes from portraits in churches and homes. I know
this couldn't possibly bear resemblance to the
historical Jesus. Stories like today's from the Gospel
of Mark challenge that vision of Jesus in pristine
perfection, as he spits and touches strangers. He
wasn't afraid to get dirty. We, too, may need to get
dirty when we lift up others as Jesus did. We know
that Jesus will not reject us, no matter what we look
like when we approach.

Genesis 3:1–8
Psalm 32:1–2,5,6,7
Mark 7:31–37

FEBRUARY 16

In every age, O Lord, you have been our refuge.
—PSALM 90:1

Scripture teems with tales of disobedience and forgiveness, a reminder that God's mercy has a very long history, our refuge in every age. God never tires of welcoming us back. Even with all our foibles and flaws, the Lord is always willing to meet us and offer us a safe place of rest and love.

Genesis 3:9–24
Psalm 90:2,3–4abc,5–6,12–13
Mark 8:1–10

FEBRUARY 17

• SIXTH SUNDAY IN ORDINARY TIME •

*"Woe to you when all speak well of you,
for their ancestors treated the false prophets in this way."*
—LUKE 6:26

I don't fear receiving praise from others, but I do fear
my pursuit of it. A quip or photo might earn a lot of
"likes" or even old-fashioned laughs, but if I'm
sharing just for vanity's sake, I'm betraying myself
and my values. Self-reflection and quiet prayer help
me check in with what really matters and, in turn,
chip away at this need to impress.

Jeremiah 17:5–8
Psalm 1:1–2,3,4 and 6 (40:5a)
1 Corinthians 15:12,16–20
Luke 6:17,20–26

FEBRUARY 18

"Why do you recite my statutes,
and profess my covenant with your mouth
Though you hate discipline
and cast my words behind you?"
—PSALM 50:16–17

It does little good to speak of God unless we are
willing to live like Christ. We need to carry God's
words with us and learn how to share them by the
way we live our lives.

Genesis 4:1–15,25
Psalm 50:1 and
8,16bc–17,20–21
Mark 8:11–13

FEBRUARY 19

The disciples had forgotten to bring bread, and they had only one loaf with them in the boat.

—MARK 8:14

The disciples spend a lot of time worrying about food. They try to catch fish and they can't. Crowds grow around Jesus, and those crowds need to be fed. And in today's Gospel, they fail to bring rations with them as they travel by boat with Jesus. From a distance, it may seem silly when compared to the magnitude of Jesus' ministry, but we all know how distracting hunger can be. Jesus becomes exasperated with them when they fail to understand him, when they focus on the wrong thing. But still, he feeds them.

Genesis 6:5–8,7:1–5,10
Psalm 29:1a and 2,3ac–4,3b and 9c–10
Mark 8:14–21

When Jesus and his disciples arrived at Bethsaida, people brought to him a blind man and begged Jesus to touch him.
—MARK 8:22

So many of the stories of Jesus' healing miracles involve people bringing a sick person to Jesus. I am moved by their commitment and their willingness to beg Jesus to help their loved one. They must have been thrilled to see the sick restored to health and to see that their trust and faith in God was answered. What do you want to bring to Jesus today? Can you trust that he will listen and provide you with what you need?

Genesis 8:6–13,20–22
Psalm 116:12–13,14–15,18–19
Mark 8:22–26

FEBRUARY 21

He spoke this openly. Then Peter took him aside and began to rebuke him.
—MARK 8:32

Poor Peter, always doing something knuckleheaded. Today's reading finds him taking Jesus aside and rebuking him for talking about his impending suffering and Resurrection. I can't blame him for wanting Jesus to stop talking about suffering, and I have to laugh at his audacity in criticizing Jesus right after his great profession of faith to Jesus: "You are the Messiah" (Mark 8:29). Peter gives me hope, because Jesus continues to love his friend. If Peter can stay close to Jesus' heart and do great things for God, maybe there's hope for the rest of us impulsive talkers, too.

Genesis 9:1–13
Psalm 102:16–18,19–21,29 and 22–23
Mark 8:27–33

FEBRUARY 22

• THE CHAIR OF ST. PETER THE APOSTLE •

You spread the table before me
in the sight of my foes;
You anoint my head with oil;
my cup overflows.
—PSALM 23:5

To my husband's dismay, I am a very sloppy chef. In my excitement and eagerness to create something delicious to share, I inevitably make a mess in the kitchen. The image of the cup overflowing is a familiar one to me. Maybe God's kitchen is a little like mine, so profligate with flavor and goodness that there is rosemary on the floor, onion down in the stove burners, and, somehow, flour all over the front of the fridge.

1 Peter 5:1–4
Psalm 23:1–3a,4,5,6
Matthew 16:13–19

Faith is the realization of what is hoped for and evidence of things not seen.
—HEBREWS 11:1

I've never had a firm grasp on what this oft-quoted verse means, but I'm learning to be OK with that. Faith is important to us, so we seek an explanation. I place my hope in the mystery, knowing that I will spend the rest of my life discovering the marvelous mystery of God.

Hebrews 11:1–7
Psalm 145:2–3,4–5,10–11
Mark 9:2–13

Sunday

FEBRUARY 24

• SEVENTH SUNDAY IN ORDINARY TIME •

"To you who hear I say, love your enemies, do good to those who hate you, bless those who curse you, pray for those who mistreat you."
—LUKE 6:27–28

Jesus' instructions to the disciples to love their enemies and bless those who curse them are challenging. How difficult it can be to pray for the one who hurts us. So what is it about Jesus that keeps us following him, despite such demands that go against our human nature?

1 Samuel 26:2,7–9,12–13,22–23
Psalm 103:1–2,3–4,8,10,12–13 (8a)
1 Corinthians 15:45–49
Luke 6:27–38

➢ 85 ≼

*Then the boy's father cried out, "I do believe, help
my unbelief!"*
—MARK 9:24

Today's Gospel reading acknowledges the
complexity of our hearts, that we hold belief and
doubt together. Rather than analyze where one ends
and the other begins, try offering them both to God
today and join your prayer to that of the sick boy's
father: "I do believe, help my unbelief!"

Sirach 1:1–10
Psalm 93:1ab,1cd–2,5
Mark 9:14–29

FEBRUARY 26

Accept whatever befalls you,
when sorrowful, be steadfast,
and in crushing misfortune be patient;
For in fire gold and silver are tested,
and worthy people in the crucible of humiliation.
—SIRACH 2:4–5

When I was diagnosed with chronic illness, it took me a long time to shake the emotional pain that came with the new physical pain. I clung to my inner hurt because I feared that if I weren't upset, God wouldn't know how badly I wanted to be healed. By consistently turning to prayer, even with resentment in my heart, I couldn't help but see that God loved me and knew my pain. I didn't need to cling to my woundedness to make it known. Is there misfortune you are struggling to accept? Is it holding you back?

Sirach 2:1–11
Psalm 37:3–4,18–19,27–28,39–40
Mark 9:30–37

FEBRUARY 27

*Jesus replied, "Do not prevent him. There is no one who
performs a mighty deed in my name who can at the same time
speak ill of me. For whoever is not against us is for us."*

—MARK 9:39–40

Jesus criticizes the disciples' desire to prevent
outsiders from acting in his name. Are there people
doing good works in your life whose goodness you
fail to see? Or whose goodness you may not want
to see?

Sirach 4:11–19
Psalm 119:165,168,171,172,174,175
Mark 9:38–40

FEBRUARY 28

He is like a tree
planted near running water,
That yields its fruit in due season,
and whose leaves never fade.
Whatever he does, prospers.
—PSALM 1:3

I have a shamrock plant that sits above my kitchen sink. Every time it goes dormant, I worry that it's dying. But the plant is really preparing itself to produce rich green leaves and white flowers when the time is right. The fallow seasons of our spiritual lives may seem dead, but if we remain close to our spiritual nourishment, we will yield fruit in due season.

Sirach 5:1–8
Psalm 1:1–2,3,4 and 6
Mark 9:41–50

A faithful friend is a sturdy shelter;
he who finds one finds a treasure.
—SIRACH 6:14

When I consider the friends I have made over the
years, I am astonished by their many gifts. They are
bold, adventurous, creative, and always giving of
themselves. They help me understand the
communion of saints and the body of Christ. I give
gratitude and glory to God for the abundance of
faithful friends in my life and in the world. What
friends in your life offer you a sturdy shelter? Who
in your life is a treasure?

Sirach 6:5–17
Psalm 119:12,16,18,27,34,35
Mark 10:1–12

Then he embraced the children and blessed them, placing his hands on them.
—MARK 10:16

Over and over we see Jesus welcoming whomever comes to him. Today, can we resist the impulse to exclude and instead be more like Jesus?

Sirach 17:1–15
Psalm 103:13–14,15–16,17–18
Mark 10:13–16

Sunday

MARCH 3

• EIGHTH SUNDAY IN ORDINARY TIME •

The fruit of a tree shows the care it has had;
so too does one's speech disclose the bent of one's mind.
—SIRACH 27:6

If you're like me, you may find that the sins that
tempt you most are those that involve speech: I
gossip and make careless remarks far too often.
Avoiding these sins is a lifelong struggle, which
begins in my mind. By disciplining my thoughts and
thinking well of people, it is easier for me to speak
well of them—and of the world.

Sirach 27:4–7
Psalm 92:2–3,13–14,15–16
1 Corinthians 15:54–58
Luke 6:39–45

MARCH 4

• ST. CASIMIR •

Return to him and give up sin,
pray to the LORD and make your offenses few.
—SIRACH 17:20

We can hear with confidence the Lord's command to
repent, because we know we will be forgiven and
truly loved by the one whose love is everlasting.
When you are called to change, even if it is change
that will make you uncomfortable, have faith in such
everlasting love. Our repentance helps us offer an
authentic response to God's love.

Sirach 17:20–24
Psalm 32:1–2,5,6,7
Mark 10:17–27

MARCH 5

"But many that are first will be last, and the last will be first."
—MARK 10:31

Jesus has a way of upending our expectations. Pray
with that idea as we prepare for Lent: Are there
expectations you need to abandon? Can you use the
upcoming season to shake up your life and be
made new?

Sirach 35:1–12
Psalm 50:5–6,7–8,14 and 23
Mark 10:28–31

MARCH 6

• ASH WEDNESDAY •

A clean heart create for me, O God,
and a steadfast spirit renew within me.
—PSALM 51:12

We often think of our Lenten sacrifices as a test of
our will. How steadfast and committed we can
remain. However, think not of your commitments as
a test but as a collaboration with the Lord, upon
whom we can always call to cleanse our hearts and
renew our spirits.

Joel 2:12–18
Psalm 51:3–4,5–6ab,12–13,14 and 17
2 Corinthians 5:20–6:2
Matthew 6:1–6,16–18

Thursday

MARCH 7

• SS. PERPETUA AND FELICITY, MARTYRS •

For the LORD watches over the way of the just,
but the way of the wicked vanishes.
—PSALM 1:6

St. Perpetua and her servant, St. Felicity, refused to
accept Roman gods in third-century Carthage and
were beheaded. They faced martyrdom together,
leaving us with an example of companionship as well
as sacrifice. Be on the lookout today for people who
could use your friendship or encouragement.

Deuteronomy 30:15–20
Psalm 1:1–2,3,4 and 6
Luke 9:22–25

Friday

MARCH 8

• ST. JOHN OF GOD, RELIGIOUS •

This, rather, is the fasting that I wish: / releasing those bound unjustly, /
untying the thongs of the yoke; / Setting free the oppressed, / breaking
every yoke; / Sharing your bread with the hungry, / sheltering the
oppressed and the homeless; / Clothing the naked when you see them, /
and not turning your back on your own.
—ISAIAH 58:6–7

Our Lenten fast should include fasting from selfishness,
willful ignorance, and destructive privilege. If I open my eyes
to the oppressed and homeless, I see that there is little that
divides us. I have not earned the advantages that first allowed
me to thrive. I am no better than the naked and the hungry.
Sharing my abundance and breaking apart injustices: this is
the fast that the Lord desires. May we desire the same
deep in our hearts. Even if we don't yet desire it fully, may we
continue to share our abundance.

Isaiah 58:1–9a
Psalm 51:3–4,5–6ab,18–19
Matthew 9:14–15

MARCH 9

• ST. FRANCES OF ROME, RELIGIOUS •

Jesus saw a tax collector named Levi sitting at the customs post. He said to him, "Follow me." And leaving everything behind, he got up and followed him.
—LUKE 5:27–28

I am comforted by how straightforward this story is. No matter how conflicted we may be about the sacrifices faith demands, we can always give that simple answer to Jesus' call: Yes, I will follow you.

Isaiah 58:9b–14
Psalm 86:1–2,3–4,5–6
Luke 5:27–32

MARCH 10

• FIRST SUNDAY OF LENT •

*Filled with the Holy Spirit, Jesus returned from the Jordan
and was led by the Spirit into the desert for forty days, to be
tempted by the devil. He ate nothing during those days, and
when they were over he was hungry.*

—LUKE 4:1–2

Jesus knew hunger and need just as we do. He was
not exempt from the temptations that we endure. He
had the integrity to stay true to himself in spite of
these temptations. What is tempting you today?
What helps you stay true and steadfast?

Deuteronomy 26:4–10
Psalm 91:1–2,10–11,12–13,14–15
Romans 10:8–13
Luke 4:1–13

"Then the righteous will answer him and say, 'Lord, when did
we see you hungry and feed you,
or thirsty and give you a drink?'"
—MATTHEW 25:37

Do not delay in considering these questions: Where
did you meet Jesus recently? Maybe there was a
child who needed your care, a lonely acquaintance
in need of a listening ear, or a prickly stranger who
tested your patience. Jesus associates with those in
need. Where do you meet him? How do you
serve him?

Leviticus 19:1–2,11–18
Psalm 19:8,9,10,15
Matthew 25:31–46

MARCH 12

Give us this day our daily bread.
—MATTHEW 6:11

Lord, teach me to be content with what I need for today. I fret so much about piling up resources for well into the future. But you teach us to only ask for what we need. Help us see our real needs clearly today.

Isaiah 55:10–11
Psalm 34:4–5,6–7,16–17,18–19
Matthew 6:7–15

MARCH 13

My sacrifice, O God, is a contrite spirit;
a heart contrite and humbled, O God, you will not spurn.
—PSALM 51:19

It can feel like a sacrifice to admit when we are
wrong and need forgiveness. I battle my pride every
time I have to express contrition, but I know that
doing so helps me develop a constant readiness and
willingness to change course.

Jonah 3:1–10
Psalm 51:3–4,12–13,18–19
Luke 11:29–32

MARCH 14

*Jesus said to his disciples: "Ask and it will be given to you;
seek and you will find; knock and the door will be
opened to you."*
—MATTHEW 7:7

Jesus' words here give me the courage to take my
needs to God, who waits for me and wants to give
me good things. It is not a failing or a bother to ask
for what we need. Perhaps God is even waiting for
you to ask and wondering why you haven't
knocked yet.

Esther C:12,14–16,23–25
Psalm 138:1–2ab,2cde–3,7c–8
Matthew 7:7–12

Whoever is angry with his brother will be liable to judgment.
—MATTHEW 5:22

Unfortunately, I am prone to anger. Ideally, when my anger flares, I pause and pray for whomever I am angry with. I consider all that I know about them, focusing on the good, and ask sincerely for God to bless them. No passive-aggressiveness or ulterior motives, just sincerity. Too often I fail to live up to this ideal, but I have learned it is the surest way to open my heart again.

Ezekiel 18:21–28
Psalm 130:1–2,3–4,5–7a,7bc–8
Matthew 5:20–26

MARCH 16

So be perfect, just as your heavenly Father is perfect.
—MATTHEW 5:48

Rather than be overwhelmed by the command to be perfect, consider that this high expectation indicates that Jesus believes we are capable of it. We may miss the mark most of the time, but what a glorious mark to miss!

Deuteronomy 26:16–19
Psalm 119:1–2,4–5,7–8
Matthew 5:43–48

MARCH 17

• SECOND SUNDAY OF LENT •

Join with others in being imitators of me, brothers and sisters, and observe those who thus conduct themselves according to the model you have in us.
—PHILIPPIANS 3:17

Years ago, a student asked me if I watched an especially soapy prime-time drama and was surprised when I said, "No. I try not to watch shows about people committing adultery." I wasn't trying to be preachy. Over time, I've realized that some entertainment made me feel empty, and I began to avoid it. Each of us, with attentiveness, can determine the most life-giving media "diet." This Lent, can you adjust what you consume, finding more life-giving books, movies, and other entertainment that present you with characters who are worthy of imitation?

Genesis 15:5–12,17–18
Psalm 27:1,7–8,8–9,13–14 (1a)
Philippians 3:17–4:1 or 3:20–4:1
Luke 9:28b–36

Let the prisoners' sighing come before you;
with your great power free those doomed in death.
—PSALM 79:11

God's mercy and forgiveness are a comfort when we
consider our own sins. Do I have a big enough heart
to love God's mercy as it extends to prisoners,
criminals, or people whom I have judged unworthy?
Wanting the best for those who we don't think
deserve it, and believing that they do deserve it,
makes us more like God.

Daniel 9:4b–10
Psalm 79:8,9,11 and 13
Luke 6:36–38

MARCH 19

• ST. JOSEPH, SPOUSE OF THE BLESSED VIRGIN MARY •

Such was his intention when, behold, the angel of the Lord
appeared to him in a dream and said,
"Joseph, son of David, do not be afraid to take Mary your
wife into your home. For it is through the Holy Spirit that this
child has been conceived in her."
—MATTHEW 1:20

The angel tells Joseph not to be afraid. Consider all
he would have to fear in the coming months and
years: judgment, danger, and the mystery of helping
to bring up the Son of God. I wonder if he cherished
this dream and looked back on it when life was
overwhelming. I wonder if he was able to remain
steadfast because he knew he had been chosen
and called.

2 Samuel 7:4–5a, 12–14a,16
Psalm 89:2–3,4–5,27 and 29
Romans 4:13,16–18,22
Matthew 1:16,18–21,24a or
Luke 2:41–51a

MARCH 20

*Jesus said in reply, "You do not know what you are asking.
Can you drink the chalice that I am going to drink?" They
said to him, "We can."*
—MATTHEW 20:22

Jesus never hid the fact that his way would be
painful and humiliating, yet he continued living in
service and friendship until the end. Can we hold
both of those truths in our hearts today: that life is
both sacrifice and joy?

Jeremiah 18:18–20
Psalm 31:5–6,14,15–16
Matthew 20:17–28

MARCH 21

"And he cried out, 'Father Abraham, have pity on me. Send Lazarus to dip the tip of his finger in water and cool my tongue, for I am suffering torment in these flames.'"
—LUKE 16:24

The first time I read the parable of Lazarus closely, I was shocked when the rich man spoke of Lazarus by name. He knew the poor man well enough to know his name yet had never tended to his needs. Opportunities for generosity are right in front of us. May we not let our routines or what we think is normal blind us from what we ought to do.

Jeremiah 17:5–10
Psalm 1:1–2,3,4 and 6
Luke 16:19–31

Friday

MARCH 22

When his brothers saw that their father loved him best of all his sons, they hated him so much that they would not even greet him.
—GENESIS 37:4

Envy is corrosive. I should know: I suffer from it often. By any objective measure, I have far more than I need, but I still envy people who have more of what I fear I lack: those who are better singers, better writers, better athletes; those who are more beautiful or more graceful or kinder. Decades of trying to shed this ugly trait have allowed me to feel happy for others when they shine, but I still feel that awful pang of jealousy that shames me. I invite God into that sin and shame for comfort and healing. Although I would rather not feel these things, for now the best I can do is use them as a tool to bring my needs and insecurity to prayer.

Genesis 37:3–4,12–13a,17b–28a
Psalm 105:16–17,18–19,20–21
Matthew 21:33–43,45–46

Bless the LORD, O my soul;
and all my being, bless his holy name.
—PSALM 103:1

How do I express praise not just with my mouth but
with my soul, with all my being? The words of praise
are only the beginning, and they are often the easy
part. I have to carefully tend to my spiritual life so
that my inmost self remains inclined to praise, and
my actions reflect this.

Micah 7:14–15,18–20
Psalm 103:1–2,3–4,9–10,11–12
Luke 15:1–3,11–32

Sunday

MARCH 24

• THIRD SUNDAY OF LENT •

So Moses decided, "I must go over to look at this remarkable sight, and see why the bush is not burned."
—EXODUS 3:3

Moses' curiosity led him into an exceptional conversation with God at the burning bush, which continued onward in their unique relationship. If something piques your interest today, learn more. You never know where it will lead.

Exodus 17:3–7 or 3:1–8a,13–15
Psalm 95:1–2,6–7,8–9 (8) or
103:1–2,3–4,6–7,8,11 (8a)
Romans 5:1–2,5–8 or
1 Corinthians 10:1–6,10–12
John 4:5–42 or
4:5–15,19b–26,39a,40–42 or
Luke 13:1–9

MARCH 25

• THE ANNUNCIATION OF THE LORD •

And coming to her, he said, "Hail, full of grace! The Lord
is with you."
—LUKE 1:28

Mary was "greatly troubled" by the angel's greeting. Surely she was concerned by the presence of the angel, but she also "pondered what sort of greeting this might be." Was she unaccustomed to being spoken of highly? Did she not believe she was full of grace or close to the Lord? Let us be aware that the Lord is also with us, not so that we can boast but so our response may be, like Mary's, a resounding *yes*.

Isaiah 7:10–14,8:10
Psalm 40:7–8a,8b–9,10,11
Hebrews 10:4–10
Luke 1:26–38

MARCH 26

He guides the humble to justice,
he teaches the humble his way.
—PSALM 25:9

The opening of T. E. Brown's poem "Indwelling"
illustrates the lack of self-regard that leaves us open
to learn and be filled. Brown imagines the selfless
soul as an empty shell resting on the ocean floor. It's
found by "He," who says, "This is not dead," and fills
"thee with himself instead." God teaches the humble
the way. Is it because the humble are most able to
accept guidance?

Daniel 3:25,34–43
Psalm 25:4–5ab,6 and 7bc,8–9
Matthew 18:21–35

MARCH 27

"However, take care and be earnestly on your guard not to forget the things which your own eyes have seen, nor let them slip from your memory as long as you live, but teach them to your children and to your children's children."
—DEUTERONOMY 4:9

As years go by and technology progresses, it becomes easier to capture and store memories—or at least the photos and videos that we think are memories. The memories that truly sustain us are the ones we know by heart. What are your most treasured memories? How is God revealed in them?

Deuteronomy 4:1,5–9
Psalm 147:12–13,15–16,19–20
Matthew 5:17–19

MARCH 28

If today you hear his voice, harden not your hearts.
—PSALM 95:7–8

If I do not take care of myself physically, emotionally, and spiritually, I become quick to anger and, at times, despairing and depressed. That's how my heart hardens. When your heart is hard, what emerges? How do you turn things around?

Jeremiah 7:23–28
Psalm 95:1–2,6–7,8–9
Luke 11:14–23

And when Jesus saw that he answered with understanding, he said to him, "You are not far from the Kingdom of God." And no one dared to ask him any more questions.
—MARK 12:34

The scribes had been testing Jesus with their questions. When one scribe thoughtfully commended Jesus' response, Jesus in turn responded with kindness. Often I need to reset my perspective: just because I think a conversation might be tense doesn't mean I have to be antagonistic or unkind. I should be ready to hear the goodness in what any person says.

Hosea 14:2–10
Psalm 81:6c–8a,8bc–9,10–11ab,14 and 17
Mark 12:28–34

*For it is love that I desire, not sacrifice,
and knowledge of God rather than burnt offerings.*
—HOSEA 6:6

Check in with yourself: are your Lenten sacrifices
leading you deeper into love of God and
commitment to discipleship?

Hosea 6:1–6
Psalm 51:3–4,18–19,20–21ab
Luke 18:9–14

"So he got up and went back to his father. While he was still a long way off, his father caught sight of him, and was filled with compassion. He ran to his son, embraced him and kissed him."

—LUKE 15:20

In today's Scripture reading about the prodigal son, when the father sees his son, his heart catches fire within him. Do you believe that you give God such delight? When I have trouble believing this truth, I think of this advice from the Jesuit Anthony de Mello: "Behold God beholding you . . . and smiling."

Joshua 5:9a,10–12
Psalm 34:2–3,4–5,6–7 (9a)
2 Corinthians 5:17–21
Luke 15:1–3,11–32

Lo, I am about to create new heavens
and a new earth;
The things of the past shall not be remembered
or come to mind.
—ISAIAH 65:17

When it feels as if life can't change, that our bad habits are entrenched, or that it's impossible to improve relationships, remember that God is always creating and recreating. Change and new life are always possible.

Isaiah 65:17–21
Psalm 30:2 and 4,5–6,11–12a and 13b
John 4:43–54

Tuesday

APRIL 2

• ST. FRANCIS OF PAOLA, HERMIT •

*When Jesus saw him lying there and knew that he had been ill
for a long time, he said to him, "Do you want to be well?"*
—JOHN 5:6

Yes, Lord, I want to be well. Help me not to use my
hardships as an excuse. Help me not to cling to my
flaws just because they are familiar. Heal me so that
I can be truly free.

Ezekiel 47:1–9,12
Psalm 46:2–3,5–6,8–9
John 5:1–16

Sing out, O heavens, and rejoice, O earth,
break forth into song, you mountains.
For the LORD comforts his people
and shows mercy to his afflicted.
—ISAIAH 49:13

How wonderful it is that God is always reaching out
to us! In today's reading, Isaiah commands heaven
and earth to sing out in joy over this truth. What if
we similarly devoted every utterance to honoring
the great gift of God's comfort, mercy, and presence?
How would our lives look different?

Isaiah 49:8–15
Psalm 145:8–9,13cd–14,17–18
John 5:17–30

*Our fathers made a calf in Horeb
and adored a molten image;
They exchanged their glory
for the image of a grass-eating bullock.*
—PSALM 106:19–20

What do you put above God? What do you seek
with more energy than you bring to the pursuit of a
faithful life? What do you think about more than
you think about being virtuous?

Exodus 32:7–14
Psalm 106:19–20,21–22,23
John 5:31–47

Friday

APRIL 5

• ST. VINCENT FERRER, PRIEST •

The LORD is close to the brokenhearted;
and those who are crushed in spirit he saves.
—PSALM 34:19

It is human nature to avoid pain. Sometimes we avoid things we need to do—sacrifice, hard conversations, momentous change—in an attempt to dodge suffering. If we know that God is close to the brokenhearted, why do we act like less than we are and cling to comfort at all costs?

Wisdom 2:1a,12–22
Psalm 34:17–18,19–20,21 and 23
John 7:1–2,10,25–30

⇒ 125 ∈

*The guards answered, "Never before has anyone spoken
like this man."*
—JOHN 7:46

What would it have been like to be in a crowd
listening to Jesus? What made him so remarkable?
His wisdom and eloquence? His love and attention?
How do you imagine him speaking then? What does
he look like? What is he saying? How are people
reacting? How do you hear him speaking now?

Remember not the events of the past,
the things of long ago consider not;
see, I am doing something new!
—ISAIAH 43:18–19

I have little trouble letting go of slights and insults—through blessed happenstance of personality, I am nearly incapable of holding a grudge. Unfortunately, I am obsessive over my own mistakes. In spite of growth in self-discipline and maturity, which should be pleasing to me, I tend to look back at who I was and doubt that I can be any better now. I need to let go of the judgment I feel toward the person I used to be. What do you need to let go of in order to be made new?

Isaiah 43:16–21
Psalm 126:1–2,2–3,4–5,6 (3)
Philippians 3:8–14
John 8:1–11

Jesus spoke to them again, saying, "I am the light of the world. Whoever follows me will not walk in darkness, but will have the light of life."

—JOHN 8:12

George Herbert's poem "The Call" describes Jesus as "Such a Light, as shows a feast." This light reveals all that God desires for us. All of Jesus' life, even his Passion, points toward this gift.

Daniel 13:1–9,15–17,19–30,33–62 or 13:41c–62
Psalm 23:1–3a,3b–4,5,6
John 8:12–20

From Mount Hor the children of Israel set out on the Red Sea
road, to bypass the land of Edom. But with their patience
worn out by the journey, the people complained against God
and Moses, "Why have you brought us up from Egypt to die
in this desert, where there is no food or water? We are disgusted
with this wretched food!"
—NUMBERS 21:4–5

One of the first things you learn when working in
ministry is that if the food doesn't go well at an
event, it ruins the whole thing. For better or worse,
people have been ruled by this most basic need since
the beginning of time. But we do not live by bread
alone, and the food we provide for others is often
served with the attention and care that satisfy
something deeper than physical hunger.

Numbers 21:4–9
Psalm 102:2–3,16–18,19–21
John 8:21–30

Nebuchadnezzar exclaimed, "Blessed be the God of Shadrach, Meshach, and Abednego, who sent his angel to deliver the servants who trusted in him; they disobeyed the royal command and yielded their bodies rather than serve or worship any god except their own God."
—DANIEL 3:95

My favorite children's Bible illustrated the story of Shadrach, Meshach, and Abednego—the three men who were thrown into a furnace by the king of Babylon—with a cartoon of three bearded men in robes, smiling contentedly amid flames as an angel in white stands beside them. In the fire, they do not gloat over their salvation but return to their work and to the worship of the one true God.

Daniel 3:14–20,91–92,95
Daniel 3:52,53,54,55,56
John 8:31–42

APRIL 11

• ST. STANISLAUS, BISHOP AND MARTYR •

I will maintain my covenant with you and your descendants after you throughout the ages as an everlasting pact, to be your God and the God of your descendants after you.
—GENESIS 17:7

We are blessed to have a relationship with God. None of us is alone in the covenant. Each individual is part of the people of God.

Genesis 17:3–9
Psalm 105:4–5,6–7,8–9
John 8:51–59

APRIL 12

O LORD, *my rock, my fortress, my deliverer.*
My God, my rock of refuge,
my shield, the horn of my salvation, my stronghold!
—PSALM 18:3

God is solid, unchanging, and secure. How have you
experienced God as a fortress or deliverer? In your
prayers today, imagine yourself in that firm,
safe place.

Jeremiah 20:10–13
Psalm 18:2–3a,3bc–4,5–6,7
John 10:31–42

Then the virgins shall make merry and dance,
and young men and old as well.
I will turn their mourning into joy,
I will console and gladden them after their sorrows.
—JEREMIAH 31:13

In times of sadness, Jesus' promise of joy and consolation seems impossible. But God has done the impossible by rising from the dead, so don't rule anything out.

Ezekiel 37:21–28
Jeremiah 31:10,11–12abcd,13
John 11:45–56

APRIL 14

• PALM SUNDAY OF THE PASSION OF THE LORD •

They proclaimed:
"Blessed is the king who comes
in the name of the Lord.
Peace in heaven
and glory in the highest."
—LUKE 19:38

The crowds that cheer for Jesus will soon be calling for his crucifixion. I am humbled by this, knowing that my own heart is capable of both great praise and great sin.

PROCESSION:
Luke 19:28–40

MASS:
Isaiah 50:4–7
Psalm 22:8–9,17–18,19–20,23–24 (2a)
Philippians 2:6–11
Luke 22:14—23:56 or 23:1–49

Monday

APRIL 15

• MONDAY OF HOLY WEEK •

Mary took a liter of costly perfumed oil made from genuine aromatic nard and anointed the feet of Jesus and dried them with her hair; the house was filled with the fragrance of the oil.
—JOHN 12:3

Mary's extravagant act of care for Jesus fills the entire house with the aroma of her gift. Everyone present would have been aware of her blessing. May our love of Jesus be so pervasive.

Isaiah 42:1–7
Psalm 27:1,2,3,13–14
John 12:1–11

Though I thought I had toiled in vain,
and for nothing, uselessly, spent my strength,
Yet my reward is with the LORD,
my recompense is with my God.
—ISAIAH 49:4

For many years, I have entered Holy Week worn down by my Lenten sacrifices. I always wonder if they were fruitful or if I had toiled in vain. Still, each year I come back to the practices of prayer, fasting, and almsgiving, because I know that self-discipline in these small things gives me self-discipline for big things. These practices sanctify this holy time and keep the Lord close to mind.

Isaiah 49:1–6
Psalm 71:1–2,3–4a,5ab–6ab,15 and 17
John 13:21–33,36–38

And while they were eating, he said, "Amen, I say to you, one of you will betray me."
—MATTHEW 26:21

As we move into the Triduum, reflect on the failures of the disciples. Judas is the most extreme example, yet each of the Twelve abandons Jesus in his hour of need. They are flawed humans, just as we are. Most go on to share Jesus' message heroically, despite their shortcomings.

Isaiah 50:4–9a
Psalm 69:8–10,21–22,31 and 33–34
Matthew 26:14–25

Thursday
APRIL 18

"I am the Alpha and the Omega," says the Lord God, "the one who is and who was and who is to come, the Almighty."
—REVELATION 1:8

Every diocese celebrates a Chrism Mass during Holy Week, consecrating holy oils to be used for the sacraments throughout the year. The Church prepares for another year of sanctifying her people, knowing that the Alpha and Omega remains with us until the end of time.

CHRISM MASS:
Isaiah 61:1–3a,6a,8b–9
Psalm 89:21–22,25 and 27
Revelation 1:5–8
Luke 4:16–21

EVENING MASS OF THE LORD'S SUPPER:
Exodus 12:1–8,11–14
Psalm 116:12–13,15–16bc,17–18
1 Corinthians 11:23–26
John 13:1–15

• FRIDAY OF THE PASSION OF THE LORD (GOOD FRIDAY) •

*For we do not have a high priest who is unable to sympathize
with our weaknesses, but one who has similarly been tested in
every way, yet without sin.*
—HEBREWS 4:15

Jesus submitted to every pain we might feel,
including humiliation. We do not need to fear
embarrassment or set ourselves above others because
Jesus shows us another way. Today we contemplate
his journey to death. I pray that I will leave some of
my pride in the tomb when we celebrate his return
to life.

Isaiah 52:13—53:12
Psalm 31:2,6,
12–13,15–16,17,25
Hebrews 4:14–16; 5:7–9
John 18:1—19:42

Saturday

APRIL 20

• HOLY SATURDAY •

*Hear, O Israel, the commandments of life: listen, and
know prudence!*
—BARUCH 3:9

Tonight we leave behind the sobriety of Lent and
enter into the joyousness of Easter. May we continue
the restraint and charity we have practiced during
the penitential season. May we know prudence, so
that we may continue to grow in holiness.

VIGIL:
Genesis 1:1–2:2 or 1:1,26–31a
Psalm
104:1–2,5–6,10,12,13–14,24,35 (30)
or 33:4–5,6–7,12–13,20–22 (5b)
Genesis 22:1–18 or
22:1–2,9a,10–13,15–18
Psalm 16:5,8, 9–10,11 (1)
Exodus 14:15–15:1
Exodus
15:1–2,3–4,5–6,17–18 (1b)
Isaiah 54:5–14

Psalm 30:2,4,5–6,11–12,13 (2a)
Isaiah 55:1–11
Isaiah 12:2–3,4,5–6 (3)
Baruch 3:9–15,32–4:4
Psalm 19:8,9,10,11
Ezekiel 36:16–17a, 18–28
Psalm 42:3,5,43:3,4 (42:2) or
Isaiah 12:2–3,4bcd,5–6 (3) or
Psalm 51:12–13,14–15,18–19 (12a)
Romans 6:3–11
Psalm 118:1–2,16–17,22–23
Luke 24:1–12

APRIL 21

On the first day of the week, Mary of Magdala came to the tomb early in the morning, while it was still dark, and saw the stone removed from the tomb.

—JOHN 20:1

The English translation of the Easter sequence *Victimae Paschali Laudes* includes the couplet "Speak, Mary, declaring / what you saw wayfaring." Like Mary, we are called to go forth from our Easter celebrations and allow what we now know to shine forth in our lives, and with Mary we exclaim, in the words of the sequence, "Yes, Christ my hope is arisen. Alleluia!"

Acts 10:34a,37–43
Psalm 118:1–2,16–17,22–23 (24)
Colossians 3:1–4 or 1 Corinthians 5:6b–8
John 20:1–9 or Luke 24:1–12 or, at an afternoon or evening
Mass, Luke 24:13–35

Monday

APRIL 22

And behold, Jesus met them on their way and greeted them.
They approached, embraced his feet, and did him homage.
—MATTHEW 28:9

Imagine how overwhelmed the two Marys were
when they meet Jesus while running to tell the
disciples what they had seen. Their hope in the
Resurrection is confirmed by his greeting. In the
midst of such unexpected joy, he tells them, "Do not
be afraid."

Acts 2:14,22–33
Psalm 16:1–2a and
5,7–8,9–10,11
Matthew 28:8–15

Tuesday

APRIL 23

• TUESDAY WITHIN THE OCTAVE OF EASTER •

See, the eyes of the LORD are upon those who fear him,
upon those who hope for his kindness.
—PSALM 33:18

Call to mind someone whose love of the Lord is an inspiration for you. Give thanks for his or her presence in your life. Pray for them. Consider how you can emulate them. Remember that you may be an inspiration to someone in your life as well.

Acts 2:36–41
Psalm 33:4–5,18–19,20 and 22
John 20:11–18

⇒ 143 ⇐

Wednesday

APRIL 24

• WEDNESDAY WITHIN THE OCTAVE OF EASTER •

Then they said to each other, "Were not our hearts burning within us while he spoke to us on the way and opened the Scriptures to us?"
—LUKE 24:32

When my heart catches fire with curiosity, energy, or love, I consider what God is trying to teach me in that moment. Coupled with prayer, our passions can be powerful teachers.

Acts 3:1–10
Psalm 105:1–2,3–4,6–7,8–9
Luke 24:13–35

⇒ 144 ⇐

While they were still incredulous for joy and were amazed, he
asked them, "Have you anything here to eat?"
—LUKE 24:41

After convincing the disciples he is truly present in
flesh among them, Jesus gives further evidence of his
incarnate state: he eats. In fact, Jesus eats a lot in the
post-Resurrection narratives. He feels hunger as we
do and perhaps also craves the communion that
comes from sharing food with loved ones.

Acts 3:11–26
Psalm 8:2ab and 5,6–7,8–9
Luke 24:35–48

*The stone which the builders rejected
has become the cornerstone.*
—PSALM 118:22

Even after the Resurrection, many continued to
reject Jesus through his apostles. The apostles
persevered by preaching, healing, and teaching,
fearlessly building that cornerstone upon which our
faith still stands.

Acts 4:1–12
Psalm 118:1–2 and
4,22–24,25–27a
John 21:1–14

Saturday

APRIL 27

• SATURDAY WITHIN THE OCTAVE OF EASTER •

*"It is impossible for us not to speak about what we have
seen and heard."*
—ACTS 4:20

One of my favorite hymns concludes, "If love is Lord
of heaven and earth, how can I keep from singing?"
Although my days are hectic and distractions
abound, I know I need to clear all that away to check
in with God's love, which is so transformative it is
impossible to keep it to myself.

Acts 4:13–21
Psalm 118:1 and
14–15ab,16–18,19–21
Mark 16:9–15

APRIL 28

• SECOND SUNDAY OF EASTER (OR SUNDAY OF DIVINE MERCY) •

Thomas answered and said to him, "My Lord and my God!"
—JOHN 20:28

I've never been able to think of Thomas as Doubting
Thomas. The disciples whose story he disbelieved
had hardly been at their best. Would I have believed
them? We know they were flawed. We can also
imagine how deeply Thomas loved his friend Jesus
and how Thomas was too hurt to hope that he who
was dead might have been raised. What emotion
must have overcome him when he realized it was
true: regret, maybe, but also relief, amazement, and
love. He exclaimed the only phrase that can express
the wonder he felt: my Lord and my God!

Acts 5:12–16
Psalm 118:2–4,13–15,22–24 (1)
Revelation 1:9–11a,12–13,17–19
John 20:19–31

And now, Lord, take note of their threats, and enable your
servants to speak your word with all boldness.
—ACTS 4:29

The apostles pray as their ministry grows. We can
learn from them: any effort to share God's word—be
it through ministry, child-rearing, or simply living
according to Jesus' commands—needs prayer to
flourish. St. Catherine of Siena devoted herself to a
life of prayer as a lay Dominican and, ultimately,
influenced popes and many others through her wise
counsel and piety. Never underestimate the
need for prayer.

Acts 4:23–31
Psalm 2:1–3,4–7a,7b–9
John 3:1–8

The community of believers was of one heart and mind, and no one claimed that any of his possessions was his own, but they had everything in common.
—ACTS 4:32

The communal lifestyle of the earliest Christian communities was just as remarkable in their own time as it is today. They shared and took care of one another, and "there was no needy person among them" (Acts 4:34a). When others observe our faith communities today, do they see something remarkable? What can we do to show the radical care of the first Christians?

Acts 4:32–37
Psalm 93:1ab,1cd–2,5
John 3:7b–15

"Is he not the carpenter's son?"
—MATTHEW 13:55

Mary and Joseph were ordinary. Peter, John, and the other apostles were uneducated, simple laborers. But God chose them and worked through them. The Feast of St. Joseph the Worker reminds me that holiness does not require advanced degrees or otherworldly accomplishments. It just requires a heart that loves the Lord and a commitment to live a righteous life.

Acts 5:17–26
Psalm 34:2–3,4–5,6–7,8–9
John 3:16–21 (or, for the Memorial,
Genesis 1:26–2:3 or Colossians 3:14–15,17,23–24
Psalm 90:2,3–4,12–13,14 and 16
Matthew 13:54–58)

Thursday

MAY 2

The Lord hears the cry of the poor.
—PSALM 34:7

Scripture frequently mentions the importance of caring for the poor, vulnerable, and oppressed. How hard this is to internalize in a world that encourages us to win at all costs and to disdain the losers. Even without such cultural contradiction, our own sinful hearts can lead us into selfishness. This is not the way of our God, who hears the cry of the poor and calls us to care for them.

Acts 5:27–33
Psalm 34:2 and 9,17–18,19–20
John 3:31–36

Friday

MAY 3

Their message goes out through all the earth.
—PSALM 19:5

The apostles Philip and James are remembered on
the same day because their relics both lie in the
Basilica of the Holy Apostles in Rome. They were
first linked, of course, by the call of Jesus to
discipleship and later to missionary apostleship and
martyrdom. That call to follow often brings
unexpected people into our lives. We join a
community when we follow Jesus.

1 Corinthians 15:1–8
Psalm 19:2–3,4–5
John 14:6–14

But he said to them, "It is I. Do not be afraid."
—JOHN 6:20

Jesus comforts the disciples who see him walking on
the rough sea and coming toward them. They must
have been aghast and frightened, but he dispels their
fears. When we are confronted with something
shocking, listen for the voice of Jesus saying, "It is I.
Do not be afraid."

Acts 6:1–7
Psalm 33:1–2,4–5,18–19
John 6:16–21

Sunday

MAY 5

*So the disciple whom Jesus loved said to Peter, "It is the Lord."
When Simon Peter heard that it was the Lord, he tucked in his
garment, for he was lightly clad, and jumped into the sea.*
—JOHN 21:7

Although this is uncommon in my native New
England, in some cultures the faithful don't queue for
communion but all rush forward at once. The first
time I experienced this, after I adjusted to what
looked to me like chaos, I was energized by the
image of a crowd so eager to receive. In today's
Gospel, Peter was so excited to see the Lord that he
jumped into the water to reach him. Jesus fed him
and all the others. None of those who wanted to be
near him were left hungry.

Acts 5:27–32,40b–41
Psalm 30:2,4,5–6,11–12,13 (2a)
Revelation 5:11–14
John 21:1–19 or 21:1–14

I declared my ways, and you answered me;
teach me your statutes.
Make me understand the way of your precepts,
and I will meditate on your wondrous deeds.
—PSALM 119:26–27

Learning the law of the Lord involves understanding it, living it, and loving it. This education is ongoing, and our understanding changes as we change. When I become discouraged by how much I still have to learn, I remind myself that God is always at my side, teaching me.

Acts 6:8–15
Psalm 119:23–24,26–27,29–30
John 6:22–29

So they said to Jesus, "Sir, give us this bread always."
Jesus said to them, "I am the bread of life;
whoever comes to me will never hunger, and whoever believes in
me will never thirst."
—JOHN 6:34–35

In today's reading from John, the crowd asks Jesus to prove himself, to give them a sign so they will believe. When he tells them he is the bread of life, they say, "Give us this bread always." My first reaction to this story is to think "how greedy" or "how presumptuous" of them. I've always been hesitant to make such a bold request. Yet Jesus' answer is revelatory: he says *yes*, in his way. It is worth asking for what will truly satisfy, no matter the size, especially when we direct this request to our generous God.

Acts 7:51–8:1a
Psalm 31:3cd–4,6 and 7b and
8a,17 and 21ab
John 6:30–35

Now those who had been scattered went about
preaching the word.
—ACTS 8:4

In the face of persecution and threats, the apostles
continued spreading the Good News. I imagine such
conviction and courage, and I ask myself if the
gospel and the Holy Spirit set me on fire as strongly
as they did for the apostles. What is so good about
the Good News that I can't keep from sharing it?
I search my heart for that answer.

Acts 8:1b–8
Psalm 66:1–3a,4–5,6–7a
John 6:35–40

Bless our God, you peoples,
loudly sound his praise;
He has given life to our souls,
and has not let our feet slip.
—PSALM 66:8–9

O God, who breathed life into me, may I always use
that breath to sing your praise for this singular gift.

Acts 8:26–40
Psalm 66:8–9,16–17,20
John 6:44–51

*He stayed some days with the disciples in Damascus, and he
began at once to proclaim Jesus in the synagogues, that he is
the Son of God.*
—ACTS 9:19–20

I wonder what those days were like for the
Christians after Paul's conversion. Having persecuted
Christians in the past, was he embarrassed by his
past? Were the disciples wary of his sudden change
of heart? Regardless of any tension, Paul did not let
his past hold him back. He proceeded forward,
proclaiming fullheartedly that Jesus is the Son
of God.

Acts 9:1–20
Psalm 117:1bc,2
John 6:52–59

Now in Joppa there was a disciple named Tabitha (which translated is Dorcas). She was completely occupied with good deeds and almsgiving.

—ACTS 9:36

"Completely occupied with good deeds and almsgiving" is a fine description of what discipleship looks like. Such a simple statement and way of living, yet we often make discipleship seem much more complicated. May we pray that we, too, will find ourselves completely occupied with good deeds and almsgiving.

Acts 9:31–42
Psalm 116:12–13,14–15,16–17
John 6:60–69

I, John, had a vision of a great multitude, which no one could count, from every nation, race, people, and tongue. They stood before the throne and before the Lamb, wearing white robes and holding palm branches in their hands.
—REVELATION 7:9

For many years, I took courses at a summer theology institute alongside students from around the world. A highlight of our weeks together was the time spent in worship. We brought varied customs of dance, song, gesture, and spoken prayer, and I felt enriched by the displays of faith that looked different from my own. Jesus came for people of every nation, race, and tongue. Despite our differences we come together in worship, united in Christ's love.

Acts 13:14,43–52
Psalm 100:1–2,3,5 (3c)
Revelation 7:9,14b–17
John 10:27–30

MAY 13

"If then God gave them the same gift he gave to us when we
came to believe in the Lord Jesus Christ,
who was I to be able to hinder God?"
—ACTS 11:17

In today's reading, we see Peter, a devoted Jew,
surprised that the Holy Spirit is working among the
Gentiles. Peter comes to understand that this is
God's will and that his presumptions should be laid
aside. Sometimes we participate in God's work
merely by getting out of the way.

Acts 11:1–18
Psalm 42:2–3; 43:3,4
John 10:1–10

MAY 14

• ST. MATTHIAS, APOSTLE •

"This is my commandment: love one another as I love you."
—JOHN 15:12

"Love one another as I love you." How many times have you heard this phrase? Dozens? Hundreds? It should continue to instruct us, no matter how often it is repeated. How will you let Jesus' words change you today?

Acts 1:15–17,20–26
Psalm 113:1–2,3–4,5–6,7–8
John 15:9–17

Wednesday

MAY 15

May the peoples praise you, O God;
may all the peoples praise you!
—PSALM 67:6

St. Isidore the Farmer was a simple laborer from
Madrid, who with his wife, Maria, led a life of
devotion and care for the poor. By their examples we
can learn how to better commit to lives of praise
and service.

Acts 12:24—13:5a
Psalm 67:2–3,5,6 and 8
John 12:44–50

MAY 16

"Amen, amen, I say to you, whoever receives the one I send
receives me, and whoever receives me receives the one
who sent me."
—JOHN 13:20

At times, Jesus' call for us to share his mission can feel like an impossible task. We are asked to put our needs and priorities aside and to serve as he did. In truth, what first appears to be a burden is truly a gift that he shares with us. He could constantly awe us with signs and wonders, but instead he sends his message out through unlikely messengers. Jesus trusts us to be his hands on earth. For this reason, St. Teresa of Ávila proclaimed that "Christ has no body now but yours." Accept this responsibility and consider the magnitude of this gift.

Acts 13:13–25
Psalm 89:2–3,21–22,25 and 27
John 13:16–20

"In my Father's house there are many dwelling places. If there were not, would I have told you that I am going to prepare a place for you?"
—JOHN 14:2

I cling to this verse from John when grief overtakes me. Jesus' words of comfort protect me from the fear that those I love have been lost to me forever. There is plenty of room in God's house, and room in my heart for the hope that we will be reunited there.

Acts 13:26–33
Psalm 2:6–7,8–9,10–11ab
John 14:1–6

Saturday

MAY 18

• ST. JOHN I, POPE AND MARTYR •

*All the ends of the earth have seen
the saving power of God.*
—PSALM 98:3

In modern times, we know the limits of the "ends of
the earth." We have maps, telescopes, and access to
images from all over the universe. Consider the
mystery that the psalmist expresses: salvation
permeates all of creation. Are there hidden places
you think it can't reach? Perhaps even in yourself?
Welcome God into those spaces.

Acts 13:44–52
Psalm 98:1,2–3ab,3cd–4
John 14:7–14

Sunday

MAY 19

• FIFTH SUNDAY OF EASTER •

*"This is how all will know that you are my disciples, if you
have love for one another."*
—JOHN 13:35

I read religious books, participate in liturgical
ministry, educate young people in religion, and wear
religious jewelry. I like to think that all aspects of my
life point to my faith. But none of those signifiers
matter if I do not live out Jesus' commandment of
love. As the hymn of the same name states, "They'll
know we are Christians by our love."

Acts 14:21–27
Psalm 145:8–9,10–11,12–13
Revelation 21:1–5a
John 13:31–33a,34–35

Not to us, O LORD, not to us
but to your name give glory.
—PSALM 115:1

When I focus on my own "glory" or reputation, I lose
perspective and am easily agitated. The praise of
others is fickle, and the temptation to sacrifice my
integrity to earn praise is great. But when I recognize
my tiny role in God's creation, I can participate more
freely in it. This is not self-denigration but a realistic
perspective about the vastness of creation. My place
in the world may be small, but it was a place made
just for me. Being comfortable in that role is a
collaboration with the Lord who creates all things,
who loves us enough to make us who we are, and
who truly deserves to be given glory.

Acts 14:5–18
Psalm 115:1–2,3–4,15–16
John 14:21–26

Tuesday

MAY 21

• ST. CHRISTOPHER MAGALLANES, PRIEST, AND COMPANIONS, MARTYRS •

*And when they arrived, they called the Church together and
reported what God had done with them and how he had
opened the door of faith to the Gentiles. Then they spent no
little time with the disciples.*
—ACTS 14:27–28

Paul and Barnabas tell the community at Antioch
about their travels and ministry. The community
shares in their excitement and pleasure. These
accomplished missionaries do not set themselves
above the community but spend time with their
fellow Christians.

Acts 14:19–28
Psalm 145:10–11,12–13ab,21
John 14:27–31a

"By this is my Father glorified, that you bear much fruit and become my disciples."
—JOHN 15:8

In T. S. Eliot's *Choruses from the Rock,* he writes, "The soul of man must quicken to creation." Too often we limit our vision of creativity to arts and crafts. But we also express ourselves in family life, letter writing, event planning, and countless other ways. How do you see yourself called to creativity in this phase of your life? And will you echo Eliot's words from the same poem: "Lord, shall we not bring these gifts to Your service?"

Acts 15:1–6
Psalm 122:1–2, 3–4ab, 4cd–5
John 15:1–8

MAY 23

*The whole assembly fell silent, and they listened while Paul
and Barnabas described the signs and wonders God had
worked among the Gentiles through them.*

—ACTS 15:12

The early Church resolved a dispute over inclusion
in the community at the Council of Jerusalem. The
Acts of the Apostles describes discussion and
prayerful listening as the path to resolution. When
we encounter conflict, may we be mindful that
listening is as valuable as self-expression.

Acts 15:7–21
Psalm 96:1–2a,2b–3,10
John 15:9–11

Friday

MAY 24

I will give thanks to you among the peoples, O LORD,
I will chant your praise among the nations.
—PSALM 57:10

When I lead music in the liturgy, which I do multiple times each weekend, my priority is not to show off my skill or draw attention; my focus is on encouraging the song of the assembly. My greatest hope is that my voice will be unnecessary as the leader of song. My voice of praise is only one among all people and all nations. All together, our joyful noise gives glory to God's name.

Acts 15:22–31
Psalm 57:8–9,10 and 12
John 15:12–17

Saturday

MAY 25

• ST. BEDE THE VENERABLE, PRIEST AND DOCTOR OF THE CHURCH *
ST. GREGORY VII, POPE * ST. MARY MAGDALENE DE'PAZZI, VIRGIN •

"If you belonged to the world, the world would love its own;
but because you do not belong to the world, and I have chosen
you out of the world, the world hates you."
—JOHN 15:19

To my knowledge, I haven't faced hatred for my
attempts to belong to Jesus instead of to the world,
but I have experienced judgment and
misunderstanding, which can lead to embarrassment.
It takes daily recommitment to resist the call of
worldly values and to stand firm in our convictions.

Acts 16:1–10
Psalm 100:1b–2,3,5
John 15:18–21

MAY 26

• SIXTH SUNDAY OF EASTER •

The city had no need of sun or moon to shine on it, for the glory of God gave it light, and its lamp was the Lamb.
—REVELATION 21:23

I have lived in an urban setting for more than a decade. When I visit my childhood home in a rural area, devoid of the light pollution to which I have become accustomed, I am astonished at how much brighter the stars seem. This consoles me when I am going through dark periods and the light of Christ feels distant. The deepest darkness can reveal flashes of great radiance.

Acts 15:1–2,22–29
Psalm 67:2–3,5,6,8 (4)
Revelation 21:10–14,22–23
John 14:23–29

"When the Advocate comes whom I will send you from the Father, the Spirit of truth who proceeds from the Father, he will testify to me. And you also testify, because you have been with me from the beginning."
—JOHN 15:26–27

When St. Augustine of Canterbury was on his way to evangelize England, he turned back to Rome to tell Pope Gregory I that he and his fellow monks were frightened of the difficult journey and the cruel reputation of the Angles; they were too scared to complete their task. The pope sent them right back, and they had success in their work. We are all called to put aside our fear and testify.

Acts 16:11–15
Psalm 149:1b–2,3–4,5–6a and 9b
John 15:26–16:4a

MAY 28

But Paul shouted out in a loud voice, "Do no harm to
yourself; we are all here."
—ACTS 16:28

A powerful earthquake opens the jail cells that Paul
and Silas were captive in in today's reading. When
the jailer awakes and sees that the prison doors have
opened, he draws his sword, ready to kill himself,
when Paul stops him. The jailer falls to his knees and
says, "What must I do to be saved?" (Acts 16:30).
They tell him about believing in the Lord. This
makes me wonder: would the jailer have been so
eager to learn from Paul and Silas if Paul had not
shown him kindness? The powerful message of God
is well conveyed by a gracious messenger.

Acts 16:22–34
Psalm 138:1–2ab,2cde–3,7c–8
John 16:5–11

Praise the name of the LORD,
for his name alone is exalted;
His majesty is above earth and heaven.
—PSALM 148:13

Where do you struggle to see God's majesty? What parts of your life feel dark and shut out from the Lord? In whom do you struggle to see God's grace at work? Invite the Lord to give you the vision that sees grace in all things.

Acts 17:15,22–18:1
Psalm 148:1–2,11–12,13,14
John 16:12–15

Thursday

MAY 30

• THE ASCENSION OF THE LORD •

As he blessed them he parted from them and was taken up to heaven.
—LUKE 24:51

The disciples experienced great upheaval in the weeks leading up to the Ascension. After sorrow, fear, joy, and confusion, they are left with the task of witnessing to Jesus' Resurrection with no instructions to follow. Despite this, Jesus' Ascension leaves them with "great joy," and they praise him. Sometimes, even though the way ahead is not clear, we can let faith be our navigator.

THE ASCENSION OF THE LORD:
Acts 1:1–11
Psalm 47:2–3,6–7,8–9 (6)
Ephesians 1:17–23 or
Hebrews 9:24–28,10:19–23
Luke 24:46–53

EASTER WEEKDAY:
Acts 18:1–8
Psalm 98:1,2–3ab,3cd–4
John 16:16–20

Friday

MAY 31

• THE VISITATION OF THE BLESSED VIRGIN MARY •

Shout for joy, O daughter Zion!
Sing joyfully, O Israel!
Be glad and exult with all your heart,
O daughter Jerusalem!
—ZEPHANIAH 3:14

Unfortunately, impulse control is an area of weakness
for me. Ever since my youth, I've been one to chime in
or shout out, and I'm often scolded for being too loud.
I am comforted by Mary's visit to Elizabeth and that
neither of them can contain herself. Elizabeth cries out
her blessing, and Mary proclaims the greatness of the
Lord. Their excited utterances convince me that even
my qualities that are most often criticized can be put
to good use.

Zephaniah 3:14–18a or
Romans 12:9–16
Isaiah 12:2–3,4bcd,5–6
Luke 1:39–56

JUNE 1

• ST. JUSTIN, MARTYR •

*He began to speak boldly in the synagogue; but when Priscilla
and Aquila heard him, they took him aside and explained to
him the Way of God more accurately. And when he wanted to
cross to Achaia, the brothers encouraged him and wrote to the
disciples there to welcome him. After his arrival he gave great
assistance to those who had come to believe through grace.*

—ACTS 18:26–27

The earliest Christian communities practiced radical
inclusion. In today's reading, a Jewish man named
Apollos arrives in Ephesus and starts preaching with
incomplete understanding. Established leaders
correct and instruct him privately. They encourage
him to continue preaching. They are not possessive
of their knowledge and mission. They welcome
anyone to share in it.

Acts 18:23–28
Psalm 47:2–3,8–9,10
John 16:23b–28

Sunday

JUNE 2

• THE ASCENSION OF THE LORD • SEVENTH SUNDAY OF EASTER •

*Then he fell to his knees and cried out in a loud voice, "Lord,
do not hold this sin against them"; and when he said this,
he fell asleep.*
—ACTS 7:60

C. S. Lewis writes in *The Weight of Glory*, "To be a
Christian means to forgive the inexcusable, because
God has forgiven the inexcusable in you." If there is
someone you struggle to forgive, can you allow your
heart to soften toward him or her today? If the
person you struggle to forgive is you, be gentle and
remember God's unconditional love for you.

SEVENTH SUNDAY OF EASTER:
Acts 7:55–60
Psalm 97:1–2,6–7,9 (1a, 9a)
Revelation 22:12–14,16–17,20
John 17:20–26

THE ASCENSION OF THE LORD
Acts 1:1–11
Psalm 47:2–3,6–7,8–9 (6)
Ephesians 1:17–23 or
Hebrews 9:24–28,10:19–23
Luke 24:46–53

Monday

JUNE 3

• ST. CHARLES LWANGA AND COMPANIONS, MARTYRS •

"I have told you this so that you might have peace in me. In the world you will have trouble, but take courage, I have conquered the world."
—JOHN 16:33

The hymn "My Song Is Love Unknown" by Samuel Crossman begins with the lines "My song is love unknown, my Savior's love to me; / Love to the loveless shown, that they might lovely be." It is this love that has conquered the world. Love is more powerful than the trouble the world throws at us, so we can face those troubles with love.

Acts 19:1–8
Psalm 68:2–3ab,4–5acd,6–7ab
John 16:29–33

JUNE 4

Blessed day by day be the Lord,
who bears our burdens; God, who is our salvation.
—PSALM 68:20

When my chronic illness was flaring and the pain
was debilitating, a greater burden than my pain was
my disappointment in not being able to do the
things I had always done. I felt that I was letting
everyone down because I couldn't be active. But the
people closest to me, whose love was constant
during my illness, gave me a glimpse of the love of
God. They knew and loved the very core of me,
which lay deep beneath any accomplishments,
accolades, or energy. There is more to me than what
I have done. My value is not in what I achieve but in
being a beloved child of God.

Acts 20:17–27
Psalm 68:10–11,20–21
John 17:1–11a

They were all weeping loudly as they threw their arms around Paul and kissed him, for they were deeply distressed that he had said that they would never see his face again. Then they escorted him to the ship.

—ACTS 20:37–38

The community of Ephesus laments as they say farewell to Paul. He is leaving for Jerusalem, where he expects "imprisonment and hardships." But they do not cling or hold him back as he follows the urging of the Holy Spirit. They let him go freely, trusting he is doing the work of God. We, too, must trust when someone's vocation challenges our desire to keep our loved ones near us. We trust God's call, and we trust the listening heart of the one we love.

Acts 20:28–38
Psalm 68:29–30,33–35a,35bc–36ab
John 17:11b–19

JUNE 6

• ST. NORBERT, BISHOP •

The following night the Lord stood by him and said, "Take courage. For just as you have borne witness to my cause in Jerusalem, so you must also bear witness in Rome."
—ACTS 23:11

In today's reading, the Lord encourages Paul and tells him that his work is not done. May we pray to accept God's encouragement when we're weary, even if it does not come with a promise of rest.

Acts 22:30,23:6–11
Psalm 16:1–2a and
5,7–8,9–10,11
John 17:20–26

He said to him the third time, "Simon, son of John, do
you love me?"
—JOHN 21:17

Jesus gives Peter three opportunities to express his
love, each time replying with instructions to care for
his flock. We all have limitless chances to express
our love of Jesus in prayer. We can also turn the
question around, asking Jesus, "Do you love me?"
with confidence that the answer will be "Yes, of
course. Always, I love you."

Acts 25:13b–21
Psalm 103:1–2,11–12,19–20ab
John 21:15–19

There are also many other things that Jesus did, but if these were to be described individually, I do not think the whole world would contain the books that would be written.
—JOHN 21:25

Speaking about God is like talking about falling in love: there is always more to say. You could go on and on and never exhaust the topic. You know all your words cannot perfectly capture what you're trying to express, but you also know that this indescribability is part of its magnificence. Whether your prayer today is verbose or wordless, know that it is enough.

Acts 28:16–20,30–31
Psalm 11:4,5 and 7
John 21:20–25

Sunday

JUNE 9

• PENTECOST SUNDAY •

*To each individual the manifestation of the Spirit is given
for some benefit.*
—1 CORINTHIANS 12:7

I don't need to do everything to spread the Good
News. The Spirit inspires each member of Christ's
body to serve in his or her unique fashion. I can do
what my part of the body is meant to do. I
acknowledge my need for the gifts of others and our
shared reliance on the abundant Spirit of God.

VIGIL:
Genesis 11:1–9 or Exodus 19:3–8a,16–20b or
Ezekiel 37:1–14 or Joel 3:1–5
Psalm 104:1–2,24,35,27–28,29,30
Romans 8:22–27
John 7:37–39

DAY:
Acts 2:1–11
Psalm 104:1,24,29–30,31,34
1 Corinthians 12:3b–7,12–13 or Romans 8:8–17
John 20:19–23 or 14:15–16,23b–26

Monday

JUNE 10

"Glorious things are told of you,
O city of God.
—PSALM 87:3

What does church mean to you? Is it a place? A
community? A feeling? Today's feast reminds me that
the Church is made up of the people of God, under
the care of Mary. The people of God include those
with whom I disagree. They include those who make
me angry or afraid. But Mary's worldwide care for all
calls us to a challenging worldwide love. Today in
prayer, remember those whom you struggle to love,
and place them before our loving mother in
your heart.

Genesis 3:9–15,20 or
Acts 1:12–14
Psalm 87:1–2,3 and 5,6–7
John 19:25–34

Tuesday

JUNE 11

• ST. BARNABAS, APOSTLE •

"You are the light of the world."
—MATTHEW 5:14

You are the light of the world. Yes, you. Each of us
has a share in Jesus' illuminating mission. Whether
this feels like a gift or a burden today, let your
light shine.

Acts 11:21b–26,13:1–3
Psalm 98:1,2–3ab,3cd–4,5–6
Matthew 5:13–16

Wednesday

JUNE 12

*Extol the LORD, our God,
and worship at his holy mountain;
for holy is the LORD, our God.*
—PSALM 99:9

God spoke to Moses on the holy mountain of
Mount Sinai. Where are the holy mountains in your
life? Where have you clearly heard God's voice? The
Word comes to us in churches and canyons,
bedrooms and hospital rooms. There is nowhere that
we cannot pray, and no place that cannot be
made holy.

2 Corinthians 3:4–11
Psalm 99:5,6,7,8,9
Matthew 5:17–19

Thursday

JUNE 13

• ST. ANTHONY OF PADUA, PRIEST AND DOCTOR OF THE CHURCH •

Now the Lord is the Spirit and where the Spirit of the Lord is,
there is freedom.
—2 CORINTHIANS 3:17

I feel most free when I am with people who love and
understand me. I am comfortable sharing my ideas
and enthusiasms. I don't fear their judgment, and I
can make mistakes without embarrassment. I know
they want what is best for me and will help me when
I need it. If I find such love and freedom in my
family and friends, how much more is there to be
found in God's loving presence?

2 Corinthians 3:15–4:1,3–6
Psalm 85:9ab and
10,11–12,13–14
Matthew 5:20–26

Friday

JUNE 14

We hold this treasure in earthen vessels, that the surpassing power may be of God and not from us.
—2 CORINTHIANS 4:7

When I became very sick at age 30, it was an existential shock. I had never been seriously ill before. No one in my close family had a chronic illness. Health was part of my identity. Intellectually I knew that my body was vulnerable, but a diagnosis was what really forced me to confront the fragility of human flesh. The body is a humble vessel, made glorious by the Lord. When it suffers, it bears witness to Christ's suffering. And just like Christ, these confounding, miraculous bodies will be raised on the last day.

2 Corinthians 4:7–15
Psalm 116:10–11,15–16,17–18
Matthew 5:27–32

Saturday
JUNE 15

"Let your 'Yes' mean 'Yes,' and your 'No' mean 'No.'
Anything more is from the Evil One."
—MATTHEW 5:37

In today's reading, Jesus tells his disciples never to take oaths on heaven or earth but to keep their agreements simple and transparent. How does this instruction make you feel? Does the prospect of such honest plainspokenness fill you with anxiety? Or with relief?

2 Corinthians 5:14–21
Psalm 103:1–2,3–4,9–10,11–12
Matthew 5:33–37

Sunday

JUNE 16

• THE MOST HOLY TRINITY •

Thus says the wisdom of God:
"The LORD possessed me, the beginning of his ways,
the forerunner of his prodigies of long ago;
from of old I was poured forth,
at the first, before the earth."
—PROVERBS 8:22–23

The wisdom of God has always been with us. The
ability to contemplate such things is a hallmark of
humanity. Sometimes our inner lives can cause pain.
Remember that intellect and emotion are gifts of
God, allowing us to think and to understand and
helping us to pray.

Proverbs 8:22–31
Psalm 8:4–5,6–7,8–9 (2a)
Romans 5:1–5
John 16:12–15

For he says:
In an acceptable time I heard you,
and on the day of salvation I helped you.
Behold, now is a very acceptable time;
behold, now is the day of salvation.
—2 CORINTHIANS 6:2

I once received the following advice as an educator:
give students a few minutes to start homework in
class, because sometimes getting started can seem
like such an obstacle that they may give up if they
have to do it on their own. Isn't that also true of
adults? We want to do good things and be better
people, but how can we even start? Now is the time.
Decide and begin. We always have God by our side,
helping us begin and letting us know that we're
not alone.

2 Corinthians 6:1–10
Psalm 98:1,2b,3ab,3cd–4
Matthew 5:38–42

JUNE 18

The LORD protects strangers.
—PSALM 146:9

My failures of charity often come not from
stinginess but from fear. It may be fear of saying the
wrong thing, or being misunderstood, or having to
interact with a stranger. Pope Francis tweeted on
September 21, 2013, that "true charity requires
courage: Let us overcome our fear of getting our
hands dirty so as to help those in need." Today we
pray to not let fear impede our desire to reach out.

2 Corinthians 8:1–9
Psalm 146:2,5–6ab,6c–7,8–9a
Matthew 5:43–48

$\mathcal{W}ednesday$

JUNE 19

Brothers and sisters, consider this: whoever sows sparingly will also reap sparingly, and whoever sows bountifully will also reap bountifully. Each must do as already determined, without sadness or compulsion, for God loves a cheerful giver.
—2 CORINTHIANS 9:6–7

Is there something you could give more bountifully? Attention, patience, compliments, or even money? If there is an area of your life in which you're holding back, consider whether giving more freely would make you feel freer. God loves a cheerful giver.

2 Corinthians 9:6–11
Psalm 112:1bc–2,3–4,9
Matthew 6:1–6,16–18

JUNE 20

Jesus said to his disciples: "In praying, do not babble like the pagans, who think that they will be heard because of their many words. Do not be like them. Your Father knows what you need before you ask him."
—MATTHEW 6:7–8

I admit I'm guilty of babbling in prayer. I love words, and I use them to understand what is stirring in my heart. But God does not need those words to know me and my needs. The words are my personal expression, a response to the love and care that constantly flow toward me from heaven.

2 Corinthians 11:1–11
Psalm 111:1b–2,3–4,7–8
Matthew 6:7–15

Friday

JUNE 21

• ST. ALOYSIUS GONZAGA, RELIGIOUS •

*"The lamp of the body is the eye. If your eye is sound, your
whole body will be filled with light; but if your eye is bad,
your whole body will be in darkness. And if the light in you is
darkness, how great will the darkness be."*
—MATTHEW 6:22–23

People frequently do just what we expect of them.
For instance, if we expect an argument, that's exactly
what we'll get. What if we changed what we are
looking for? What if we expect the best of people in
hopes that we can be a part of drawing their light
into the world? When we change the way we see, it
sometimes changes others, and it always changes us.

2 Corinthians 11:18,21–30
Psalm 34:2–3,4–5,6–7
Matthew 6:19–23

Saturday

JUNE 22

• ST. PAULINUS OF NOLA, BISHOP • SS. JOHN FISHER, BISHOP, AND
THOMAS MORE, MARTYRS •

*Three times I begged the Lord about this, that it might leave
me, but he said to me, "My grace is sufficient for you, for
power is made perfect in weakness." I will rather boast most
gladly of my weaknesses, in order that the power of Christ
may dwell with me.*
—2 CORINTHIANS 12:8–9

It is our need that allows God to work in us. I feel so
much pressure to appear tough, to make people
think that I can handle everything on my own and
that nothing gets to me. Of course this isn't true.
Instead of fearing weakness, can we, like Paul,
rejoice in it?

2 Corinthians 12:1–10
Psalm 34:8–9,10–11,12–13
Matthew 6:24–34

JUNE 23

For as often as you eat this bread and drink the cup, you
proclaim the death of the Lord until he comes.
—1 CORINTHIANS 11:26

Jesus is an everlasting gift, a sacrifice of love for us.
This is what he told his followers to remember: his
self-offering. No wonder so many had trouble
believing he was the Messiah. He did not glory in
triumph or earthly power but in self-sacrifice. This
sacrifice continues to feed us. What love he showed
for us then and still shows us now!

Genesis 14:18–20
Psalm 110:1,2,3,4 (4b)
1 Corinthians 11:23–26
Luke 9:11b–17

JUNE 24

• THE NATIVITY OF ST. JOHN THE BAPTIST •

It is too little, he says, for you to be my servant,
to raise up the tribes of Jacob,
and restore the survivors of Israel;
I will make you a light to the nations,
that my salvation may reach to the ends of the earth.
—ISAIAH 49:6

At one point or another, Moses, Jeremiah, and Isaiah all
protested that they didn't have what it took to be God's
messengers. John the Baptist was a similarly unlikely
prophet, born unexpectedly to a barren couple. There are
no limits to who can be a light to the nations. With God,
all things are possible.

VIGIL:
Jeremiah 1:4–10
Psalm 71:1–2,3–4a,5–6ab,15ab and 17
1 Peter 1:8–12
Luke 1:5–17

DAY:
Isaiah 49:1–6
Psalm 139:1b–3,13–14ab,14c–15
Acts 13:22–26
Luke 1:57–66,80

JUNE 25

He who walks blamelessly and does justice;
who thinks the truth in his heart
and slanders not with his tongue.
—PSALM 15:2–3

Today's reading calls us to walk blamelessly, do justice, think the truth, slander not. These are not easy to perfect, but every day that we make an attempt—even an imperfect attempt—brings us closer to the goal. Life is made up of habits that we can either indulge or challenge.

Genesis 13:2,5–18
Psalm 15:2–3a,3bc–4ab,5
Matthew 7:6,12–14

JUNE 26

*As the sun was about to set, a trance fell upon Abram, and a
deep, terrifying darkness enveloped him.*
—GENESIS 15:12

Encounters with God are not for the faint of heart,
and they do not guarantee smooth sailing. In today's
reading, a "trance fell upon Abram," and he became
enveloped in terrifying darkness. Saints throughout
the ages have told similar stories. After St. Teresa of
Calcutta's death, it was revealed that she had
experienced long stretches of spiritual emptiness.
When our souls feel dry, may we draw on the
strength of whatever closeness we once felt, or
simply take comfort in the covenant God established
with us through Abraham: to always be our God.

Genesis 15:1–12,17–18
Psalm 105:1–2,3–4,6–7,8–9
Matthew 7:15–20

JUNE 27

• ST. CYRIL OF ALEXANDRIA, BISHOP AND DOCTOR OF THE CHURCH •

*"Everyone who listens to these words of mine and acts on them
will be like a wise man who built his house on rock. The rain
fell, the floods came, and the winds blew and buffeted the
house. But it did not collapse; it had been set solidly on rock."*
—MATTHEW 7:24–25

Each time we pray, when we seek Jesus' voice and
commit to doing his will, we add more stability to
the foundations of our faith. It is ongoing
construction and something on which we can always
make progress.

Genesis 16:1–12,15–16 or
16:6b–12,15–16
Psalm 106:1b–2,3–4a,4b–5
Matthew 7:21–29

Friday

JUNE 28

• THE MOST SACRED HEART OF JESUS •

*Thus says the Lord GOD: I myself will look after and
tend my sheep.*
—EZEKIEL 34:11

Jesus' sacred heart is full of burning love for us. He
calls us to repent so that we may experience his
forgiveness and love more deeply. God has always
promised to care for us like a shepherd and to
welcome us home when we have gone astray.

Ezekiel 34:11–16
Psalm 23:1–3a,3b–4,5,6 (1)
Romans 5:5b–11
Luke 15:3–7

Saturday

JUNE 29

• SS. PETER AND PAUL, APOSTLES •

Glorify the LORD with me,
let us together extol his name.
—PSALM 34:4

How different Peter and Paul were. Peter was an impulsive rural fisherman. Paul was a smooth-talking Roman citizen. Yet they both loved Jesus deeply and proclaimed his message. Who knows whom God will put in your life as a collaborator in ministry or as a partner in faith. May we all stay open to glorifying the Lord with those beside us, regardless of differences.

VIGIL:
Acts 3:1–10
Psalm 19:2–3,4–5
Galatians 1:11–20
John 21:15–19

DAY:
Acts 12:1–11
Psalm 34:2–3,4–5,6–7,8–9
2 Timothy 4:6–8,17–18
Matthew 16:13–19

Sunday

JUNE 30

• THIRTEENTH SUNDAY IN ORDINARY TIME •

For you were called for freedom, brothers and sisters. But do not use this freedom as an opportunity for the flesh; rather, serve one another through love.
—GALATIANS 5:13

Every morning, we wake up with choices. We can be pleasant or grumpy. We can be timely or rushed. We can be self-centered or give our attention to others.

Self-discipline helps us use our freedom wisely. I know for myself that I have never been disappointed by choosing service over selfishness.

1 Kings 19:16b, 19–21
Psalm 16:1–2,5,7–8,9–10,11
Galatians 5:1,13–18
Luke 9:51–62

Monday

JULY 1

• ST. JUNÍPERO SERRA, PRIEST •

Then Abraham drew nearer to him and said: "Will you sweep
away the innocent with the guilty?"
—GENESIS 18:23

In today's reading from Genesis, the Lord tells
Abraham that the cities of Sodom and Gomorrah
will not be destroyed if there are even ten righteous
people in it. "Collateral damage" is not acceptable to
the Lord. God is merciful and will let evil remain so
as not to damage the good. That means we have to
guard against evil, and we will be given the
opportunity to repent and take our place among
those who do God's will.

Genesis 18:16–33
Psalm 103:1b–2,3–4,8–9,10–11
Matthew 8:18–22

Tuesday

JULY 2

The men were amazed and said, "What sort of man is this,
whom even the winds and the sea obey?"
—MATTHEW 8:27

You have followed Jesus onto a boat, where he rests.
Without warning, the boat begins to shake. You are
thrown around on the deck. Waves drench and
pummel you. Water is in your nose and mouth, and
you struggle to stand. You stumble over to Jesus and
wake him with your cries for help. He seems to snap
at you for having little faith. But then he snaps at the
waters to be calm, and they obey. The entire created
world obeys his commands. What relief and wonder
you feel. What sort of man is this?

Genesis 19:15–29
Psalm 26:2–3,9–10,11–12
Matthew 8:23–27

You are no longer strangers and sojourners, but you are fellow citizens with the holy ones and members of the household of God, built upon the foundation of the Apostles and prophets, with Christ Jesus himself as the capstone.
—EPHESIANS 2:19–20

As members of the household of God, we are united with those who we love and those who have gone before. We carry them in our hearts and can ask for their prayers. St. Thomas, you who loved Jesus dearly and followed him so many years ago, pray that we, too, may be devoted disciples.

Ephesians 2:19–22
Psalm 117:1bc,2
John 20:24–29

Thursday

JULY 4

*Then God said: "Take your son Isaac, your only one, whom
you love, and go to the land of Moriah. There you shall offer
him up as a burnt offering on a height that I will point
out to you."*
—GENESIS 22:2

Some things are too horrible to contemplate. Words
fail, and all we can do is sit with the story in
wordless confusion and pain. This is what the story
in today's reading about Abraham and Isaac stirs in
me: terror and anguish. Yet, at the end of the story,
Abraham, Isaac, and the servants all return home
together in the shadow of God's promise of
blessings. Imagine the blessings that are waiting for
you when you trust.

Genesis 22:1b–19
Psalm 115:1–2,3–4,5–6,8–9
Matthew 9:1–8

⇒ 215 ⇐

Friday

JULY 5

He heard this and said, "Those who are well do not need a physician, but the sick do. Go and learn the meaning of the words, I desire mercy, not sacrifice. I did not come to call the righteous but sinners."
—MATTHEW 9:12–13

Knowing our brokenness, Jesus came into the world to offer healing and mercy. He came to call sinners, meaning he came to call all of us.

Genesis 23:1–4,19,24:1–8,62–67
Psalm 106:1b–2,3–4a,4b–5
Matthew 9:9–13

• ST. MARIA GORETTI, VIRGIN AND MARTYR •

Praise the name of the LORD;
Praise, you servants of the LORD
Who stand in the house of the LORD,
in the courts of the house of our God.
—PSALM 135:1–2

I often quip that I have to be careful not to talk
about Jesus as if he's not in the room. I use words too
casually and can easily forget this truth: all of the
earth is God's home.

Genesis 27:1–5,15–29
Psalm 135:1b–2,3–4,5–6
Matthew 9:14–17

Sunday

JULY 7

• FOURTEENTH SUNDAY IN ORDINARY TIME •

Let all the earth cry out to God with joy.
—PSALM 66:1

Joyce Kilmer's poem "Trees" concludes, "Poems are made by fools like me / but only God can make a tree." The abundant life of the created world gives glory to God. Nature blesses us and cries out to God with joy. We write songs, poems, and prayers to express what the trees and flowers do by merely living. Our own flourishing gives glory to God as well.

Isaiah 66:10–14c
Psalm 66:1–3,4–5,6–7,16,20 (1)
Galatians 6:14–18
Luke 10:1–12,17–20 or 10:1–9

⇒ 218 ⇐

She said to herself, "If only I can touch his cloak, I shall be cured." Jesus turned around and saw her, and said, "Courage, daughter! Your faith has saved you." And from that hour the woman was cured.
—MATTHEW 9:21–22

There is much to admire in the woman with the hemorrhage. She had endured twelve years of a health condition that left her ritually impure and ostracized. She pursued Jesus on her own, desiring just to be close enough to touch him. Jesus told her, "Your faith has saved you." How do you express your faith and desire for closeness to Jesus? What would it mean if you heard him say in return, "Your faith has saved you"?

Genesis 28:10–22a
Psalm 91:1–2,3–4,14–15ab
Matthew 9:18–26

Tuesday

JULY 9

• ST. AUGUSTINE ZHAO RONG, PRIEST, AND COMPANIONS, MARTYRS •

Hide me in the shadow of your wings.
I in justice shall behold your face;
on waking, I shall be content in your presence.
—PSALM 17:8,15

Do you ever feel a longing to hide under God's
wings? What practices do you have to make yourself
aware of God's presence? For some it is a physical
practice such as walking or deep breathing. We can
also experience the divine in visual art, music,
poetry, and sacred spaces. We believe we are in
God's loving presence; sometimes we must call on
our senses to deepen that awareness.

Genesis 32:23–33
Psalm 17:1b,2–3,6–7ab,8b and 15
Matthew 9:32–38

The brothers did not know, of course, that Joseph understood
what they said, since he spoke with them through an
interpreter. But turning away from them, he wept.
—GENESIS 42:23–24

God works through complex, sinful people who feel
fear and pain just as we do. Joseph weeps in the
presence of the brothers who hurt and abandoned
him. My heart is moved knowing that tearful
moments have a place in the story of salvation.

Genesis 41:55–57,42:5–7a,17–24a
Psalm 33:2–3,10–11,18–19
Matthew 10:1–7

JULY 11

• ST. BENEDICT, ABBOT •

Jesus said to his Apostles: "As you go, make this proclamation: 'The Kingdom of heaven is at hand.'"
—MATTHEW 10:7

In her book *The Monastery of the Heart*, Joan Chittister writes, "The function of Benedictine life, with its community commitment, is not to hide from the world. It is to make community for others around it, to enable others to also draw from its well." Our prayer and work should be apostolic, enriching the world however we may find it and inviting those around us to join us in the joy that comes with community.

Genesis 44:18–21,23b–29,45:1–5
Psalm 105:16–17,18–19,20–21
Matthew 10:7–15

Take delight in the LORD,
and he will grant you your heart's requests.
—PSALM 37:4

Prayer is not like a vending machine, into which you deposit the right words and from which your desired item is dispensed. Sometimes prayer satisfies by helping us see what we truly desire: contentedness in God's presence and delight in its pursuit.

Genesis 46:1–7,28–30
Psalm 37:3–4,18–19,27–28,39–40
Matthew 10:16–23

Be glad you lowly ones; may your hearts be glad!
—PSALM 69:33

George Gershwin's classic song "They Can't Take That Away from Me" lists memories of a lost love which in itself can never be lost. I think of that song when I consider joy, peace, faith, integrity, and all the other things the world cannot take away from me. So I work to cultivate those gifts, knowing they will not fail.

Genesis 49:29–32,50:15–26a
Psalm 105:1–2,3–4,6–7
Matthew 10:24–33

Sunday

JULY 14

• FIFTEENTH SUNDAY IN ORDINARY TIME •

*"For this command that I enjoin on you today is not too
mysterious or remote for you . . . No, it is something very near
to you, already in your mouths and in your hearts; you have
only to carry it out."*
—DEUTERONOMY 30:11,14

The God whom we obey is very near, inflaming our
hearts with love that steers us toward goodness.
Calm yourself as best you can today so that you can
hear the voice that encourages you in all
good things.

Deuteronomy 30:10–14
Psalm 69:14,17,30–31,33–34,36,37
Colossians 1:15–20
Luke 10:25–37

Monday

JULY 15

• ST. BONAVENTURE, BISHOP AND DOCTOR OF THE CHURCH •

*A new king, who knew nothing of Joseph, came to power
in Egypt.*
—EXODUS 1:8

There may be times when, despite hard work and
accomplishment, we find ourselves looked down on
or ignored. Although this wounds our pride, it does
not change our worth. We cannot control the
perceptions of others, so we must focus on living our
vocations with energy and honesty without regard
for what others might think.

Exodus 1:8–14,22
Psalm 124:1b–3,4–6,7–8
Matthew 10:34–11:1

JULY 16

• OUR LADY OF MOUNT CARMEL •

When the child grew, she brought him to Pharaoh's daughter,
who adopted him as her son and called him Moses; for she
said, "I drew him out of the water."
—EXODUS 2:10

After Moses was rescued by the Pharaoh's
daughter—in spite of her father's decree that every
newborn boy must be thrown into the Nile—he
enjoyed a life of great privilege. At first glance, it
seemed the threat to Moses' life gave him a better
life. Yet it was when he acknowledged his humble
roots and who he truly was that Moses became one
of God's great messengers, helping to deliver his
people. Moving "up" in the eyes of the world cannot
enrich our lives if we lose sight of our true identity
and calling.

Exodus 2:1–15a
Psalm 69:3,14,30–31,33–34
Matthew 11:20–24

JULY 17

*At that time Jesus exclaimed: "I give praise to you, Father,
Lord of heaven and earth, for although you have hidden these
things from the wise and the learned you have revealed them to
the childlike."*
—MATTHEW 11:25

Our God is a God of surprises, whose message is
given to the lowly. To pay attention to God working
in our lives is to constantly be surprised. I pray to be
childlike, humble, and curious so that my heart may
know Jesus better.

Exodus 3:1–6,9–12
Psalm 103:1b–2,3–4,6–7
Matthew 11:25–27

Thursday

JULY 18

"For my yoke is easy, and my burden is light."
—MATTHEW 11:30

Discipleship takes concentration and effort. It's not always a light burden. We are called to support those around us and to be there for others. We are called to self-discipline and to grow in holiness. Even when we are not acknowledged or thanked, we go to bed each night knowing we have emulated Christ, and perhaps we sleep a little easier.

Exodus 3:13–20
Psalm 105:1 and
5,8–9,24–25,26–27
Matthew 11:28–30

How shall I make a return to the LORD
for all the good he has done for me?
—PSALM 116:12

It is a marvel just to have been born. Life would be a
gift enough, but God piled on more blessings:
friends, family, and senses to perceive the
extravagant beauty of the world around us. There is
no way to fully make a return to the Lord for all this
good, but my soul longs to do so anyway. So I pay
attention to Jesus' words: "I desire mercy,
not sacrifice."

Exodus 11:10–12:14
Psalm 116:12–13,15 and
16bc,17–18
Matthew 12:1–8

Saturday

JULY 20

• ST. APOLLINARIS, BISHOP AND MARTYR •

This was a night of vigil for the LORD, as he led them out of the land of Egypt; so on this same night all the children of Israel must keep a vigil for the LORD throughout their generations.
—EXODUS 12:42

When my family gets together, after we have caught up on what's new, the conversation often returns to stories we've told and heard before. These stories always remind me of the length of our relationship. I get to know what family members were like before I was born, and I even get to know people I never met. Memory is precious. No wonder it is embedded in our faith. It places us in a community and makes us part of a long-standing tradition.

Exodus 12:37–42
Psalm 136:1 and
23–24,10–12,13–15
Matthew 12:14–21

⇒ 231 ⇐

Sunday

JULY 21

• SIXTEENTH SUNDAY IN ORDINARY TIME •

*The Lord said to her in reply, "Martha, Martha, you are
anxious and worried about many things. There is need of only
one thing. Mary has chosen the better part and it will not be
taken from her."*

—LUKE 10:41–42

At some point, most of us will share Martha's
experience of being "burdened with much serving."
Can we avoid the anxiety that distracts and
distresses us by returning to the feet of Jesus?
Perhaps through prayer? As St. Francis de Sales says,
"Every one of us needs half an hour of prayer every
day, except when we are busy—then we need
an hour."

Genesis 18:1–10a
Psalm 15:2–3,3–4,5 (1a)
Colossians 1:24–28
Luke 10:38–42

JULY 22

• ST. MARY MAGDALENE •

Mary Magdalene went and announced to the disciples,
"I have seen the Lord," and then reported what he told her.
—JOHN 20:18

Imagine the joy Mary of Magdala felt as she rushed
to share with the disciples the news of the risen
Lord. Surely she maintained those high spirits even
when the disciples were dismissive and disbelieving.
Is our confidence in the Lord so strong that we
continue to proclaim salvation even in the face of
discouragement?

Song of Songs 3:1–4b or
2 Corinthians 5:14–17
Psalm 63:2,3–4,5–6,8–9
John 20:1–2,11–18

JULY 23

• ST. BRIDGET, RELIGIOUS •

Moses stretched out his hand over the sea, and the LORD
swept the sea with a strong east wind throughout the night and
so turned it into dry land. When the water was thus divided,
the children of Israel marched into the midst of the sea on dry
land, with the water like a wall to their right and to their left.
—EXODUS 14:21–22

Lord, sweep away all those things that stand
between me and the goodness you have promised.
Help me to see clearly the path to you and to keep
that path clear for all those who seek you.

Exodus 14:21–15:1
Exodus 15:8–9,10 and 12,17
Matthew 12:46–50

*"But some seed fell on rich soil, and produced fruit, a hundred
or sixty or thirtyfold. Whoever has ears ought to hear."*
—MATTHEW 13:8–9

"If the grass is greener on the other side, water your
grass." We bear some responsibility for enriching the
soil of our souls. We can feed it with conversation,
art, exercise, music, and any other activity that
moves us to prayer. Think of all that can grow when
you are spiritually fed.

Exodus 16:1–5,9–15
Psalm 78:18–19,23–24,25–26,27–28
Matthew 13:1–9

"But it shall not be so among you. Rather, whoever wishes to be great among you shall be your servant; whoever wishes to be first among you shall be your slave."
—MATTHEW 20:26–27

Tradition has it that St. James evangelized what is now Spain on his travels to the Iberian Peninsula. Many now follow in his footsteps on the Camino de Santiago, a thousand-year-old pilgrimage path that ends at the Shrine of St. James in the Cathedral of Santiago de Compostela. In what ways have you journeyed to find Jesus and to share his message?

2 Corinthians 4:7–15
Psalm 126:1bc–2ab,2cd–3,4–5,6
Matthew 20:20–28

Friday

JULY 26

• SS. JOACHIM AND ANNE, PARENTS OF THE BLESSED VIRGIN MARY •

*"Honor your father and your mother, that you may have a
long life in the land which the LORD, your God, is
giving you."*
—EXODUS 20:12

The fourth commandment is often taught to
children as a call for obedience. On this Feast of
St. Joachim and St. Anne, the parents of the Blessed
Virgin Mary, I consider the many ways we honor our
own parents and grandparents. I had very little time
with my grandparents, but what I know of them are
stories of courage, such as leaving their homes to
come to America, and of the hard work it took to
provide for children while working low-wage jobs.
I hope that I honor them and their memories by
striving to live a virtuous life.

Exodus 20:1–17
Psalm 19:8,9,10,11
Matthew 13:18–23

*"He replied, 'No, if you pull up the weeds you might uproot
the wheat along with them. Let them grow together
until harvest.'"*
—MATTHEW 13:29–30

Jesus shares a parable in today's reading in which he
likens the kingdom of heaven to a man who sows
healthy seeds in his field. In the night, Jesus says, the
man's enemy comes and plants weeds throughout the
field. The servants want to tear out the weeds as
soon as they see them, but the man says to wait—let
them grow alongside until harvest. When I see
something that I want changed, my first impulse is
to do it right away, and if it is out of my control, I
whine to God like an impatient child. But God's time
is not my time. Having a calm enough spirit to let
things be for a while is an expression of trust.

Exodus 24:3–8
Psalm 50:1b–2,5–6,14–15
Matthew 13:24–30

Sunday

JULY 28

• SEVENTEENTH SUNDAY IN ORDINARY TIME •

"If you then, who are wicked, know how to give good gifts to your children, how much more will the Father in heaven give the Holy Spirit to those who ask him?"
—LUKE 11:13

I struggled for many years to accept gifts, compliments, or help, thinking I was unworthy of these things. But we are created to receive. And God is constantly giving. We learn from God's generosity that we, too, should be generous, and that accepting generosity is part of being a child of God.

Genesis 18:20–32
Psalm 138:1–2,2–3,6–7,7–8 (3a)
Colossians 2:12–14
Luke 11:1–13

*She said to him, "Yes, Lord. I have come to believe that you
are the Christ, the Son of God, the one who is coming
into the world."*
—JOHN 11:27

In today's reading about Mary and Martha, we see
that Martha believes Jesus is the Son of God, but she
also feels a familiarity with him that allows her to
speak freely. Jesus loves her and her family. She
inspires me to welcome Jesus, to rush to him in
excitement or need, to confess that he is my Savior,
and to hold nothing back from him.

Exodus 32:15–24,30–34
Psalm 106:19–20,21–22,23
John 11:19–27 or
Luke 10:38–42

Jesus dismissed the crowds and went into the house. His disciples approached him and said, "Explain to us the parable of the weeds in the field."
—MATTHEW 13:36

Throughout his ministry, Jesus drew large crowds and told them stories. We know he was holy and charismatic, and I imagine he was also fairly entertaining. He did not limit himself, however, to keeping people engaged. He fed them with the wisdom of God—a gift that has proven rapturous throughout time. How do the stories we tell reflect Jesus' words and method? Do the stories we tell with our mouths and with our lives truly edify? Or do they merely entertain?

Exodus 33:7–11,34:5b–9,28
Psalm 103:6–7,8–9,10–11,12–13
Matthew 13:36–43

*"The Kingdom of heaven is like a merchant searching for fine pearls.
When he finds a pearl of great price, he goes and sells all that he
has and buys it."*
—MATTHEW 13:45–46

St. Ignatius of Loyola searched relentlessly for that pearl of
great price. While convalescing from a war injury, he lay in bed
and dreamed alternately of imitating the saints and doing great
deeds for God and of achieving great success and the limelight
in knightly pursuits. When he realized that serving God was
what truly satisfied him, he made great sacrifices to be of
service. He renounced his former life and possessions, begged
for food, and spent months at the mercy of others. He even
had to sacrifice the companionship of his Jesuit brothers when
he sent them on arduous, dangerous journeys to "set the world
on fire." In the end, his passion for the Lord transformed not
only his life but also the world around him. On his feast day,
consider what small and big ways you, too, can set the world
on fire.

Exodus 34:29–35
Psalm 99:5,6,7,9
Matthew 13:44–46

AUGUST 1

• ST. ALPHONSUS LIGUORI, BISHOP AND DOCTOR OF THE CHURCH •

*My soul yearns and pines
for the courts of the LORD.
My heart and my flesh
cry out for the living God.*
—PSALM 84:3

The Italian bishop and artist St. Alphonsus Ligouri wrote extensively on moral theology, preaching, and the sacraments. He also wrote about music, and all of his creativity seemed to stem from one simple goal: to lead people closer to the living God. In his book *How to Converse with God*, he writes, "Acquire the habit of speaking to God as if you were alone with Him, familiarly and with confidence and love, as to the dearest and most loving of friends." What a gift to leave us with, as our hearts and flesh cry out for the living God.

Exodus 40:16–21,34–38
Psalm 84:3,4,5–6a and 8a,11
Matthew 13:47–53

• ST. EUSEBIUS OF VERCELLI, BISHOP • ST. PETER JULIAN EYMARD, PRIEST •

The LORD said to Moses, "These are the festivals of the LORD which you shall celebrate at their proper time with a sacred assembly."
—LEVITICUS 23:1,4

Our sacred cycles of time bring us back to important themes of our faith. In fallow spiritual seasons, we have Easter to remind us of new life. When our self-discipline falters, Lent can remind us of the virtues of praying and fasting. Even during these long weeks of Ordinary Time, the stories of the saints pop up to inspire us with their devotion and lives. Take the time to examine what is going on in your prayer life this season. Is it a time of excitement and hope? Of quiet and contemplation? May you find the movements in your heart alive and worth honoring, no matter what they are.

Leviticus 23:1,4–11,15–16,27,34b–37
Psalm 81:3–4,5–6,10–11ab
Matthew 13:54–58

*The fiftieth year you shall make sacred by proclaiming liberty
in the land for all its inhabitants. It shall be a jubilee for you,
when every one of you shall return to his own property, every
one to his own family estate.*

—LEVITICUS 25:10

It's hard to imagine this verse's proclamation of a
year of "reset"—when debts are forgiven, property
returned, and all captives set free. We may never see
a time on earth dedicated to such mercy, but we can
keep our hearts open to offer such forgiveness. May
we pray to develop a jubilee heart—one that we can
imagine, and one that is always ready to relinquish
and forgive.

Leviticus 25:1,8–17
Psalm 67:2–3,5,7–8
Matthew 14:1–12

Sunday

AUGUST 4

• EIGHTEENTH SUNDAY IN ORDINARY TIME •

Stop lying to one another, since you have taken off the old self with its practices and have put on the new self, which is being renewed, for knowledge, in the image of its creator.
—COLOSSIANS 3:9–10

I am fastidious about speaking the truth, but there may be unspoken untruths that I use to deceive. I may try to appear confident when I'm nervous or knowledgeable when I'm unsure. When pride tempts me to misrepresent myself, will I be secure enough to admit and present the truth?

Ecclesiastes 1:2,2:21–23
Psalm 90:3–4,5–6,12–13,14,17 (1)
Colossians 3:1–5,9–11
Luke 12:13–21

AUGUST 5

• THE DEDICATION OF THE BASILICA OF ST. MARY MAJOR •

When Jesus heard of the death of John the Baptist, he
withdrew in a boat to a deserted place by himself. The crowds
heard of this and followed him on foot from their towns.
—MATTHEW 14:13

What storm of emotion must have arisen in Jesus'
heart when he learned that John the Baptist had
died. He may have felt anger at Herod for this
unjust action, growing realization of his own fate on
earth, concern for John's disciples and loved ones,
and deep grief over the loss of someone who had
long been a part of his life. When life's tragedies
overwhelm, remember that such pain is not foreign
to our Savior. He, too, has been down this path and
come out the other end.

Numbers 11:4b–15
Psalm 81:12–13,14–15,16–17
Matthew 14:13–21

While he was praying his face changed in appearance and his clothing became dazzling white.
—LUKE 9:29

Day after day we perceive the world around us. From time to time, a flash illuminates our world and helps us see things as they truly are: gifts of God, full of grace. I hold on to these moments of seeing and attempt to stay open to this new vision.

Daniel 7:9–10,13–14
Psalm 97:1–2,5–6,9
2 Peter 1:16–19
Luke 9:28b–36

• ST. SIXTUS II, POPE, AND COMPANIONS, MARTYRS • ST. CAJETAN, PRIEST •

*She said, "Please, Lord, for even the dogs eat the scraps that
fall from the table of their masters."*
—MATTHEW 15:27

The Canaanite woman follows Jesus through the
crowd in today's reading from Matthew, begging
him to heal her daughter. Jesus does not heed her
pleas and tells her he is only there to help the truly
needy. But she doesn't stop. Not until he heals her
daughter. The Canaanite woman's bold challenge
calls on Jesus' power, insisting that there is enough
to go around. How are you called today to use your
own prophetic voice, just like the Canaanite woman?

Numbers 13:1–2,25–14:1,26–29a,34–35
Psalm 106:6–7ab,13–14,21–22,23
Matthew 15:21–28

AUGUST 8

• ST. DOMINIC, PRIEST •

*The whole congregation of the children of Israel arrived in the desert of
Zin in the first month, and the people settled at Kadesh. It was here that
Miriam died, and here that she was buried.*
—NUMBERS 20:1

Moses' sister Miriam appears throughout the long narrative
of the Exodus, first as a girl keeping an eye on her newborn
brother as he floats down the river. She leads the Israelites in
joyous song as they escape slavery and is punished with
leprosy for her jealousy toward Moses (her brothers Moses
and Aaron admirably plead for God's mercy toward her). And
in the middle of their sojourn in the desert, she dies. Aaron
dies not long after, and the book of Numbers recounts how
the people mourned for him. We know nothing of the
mourning for Miriam, of her brothers' sadness, or of the
Israelites' remembrance. What we have are these snippets of
her story, a glimpse of the part she played in the history
of salvation.

Numbers 20:1–13
Psalm 95:1–2,6–7,8–9
Matthew 16:13–23

Friday

AUGUST 9

• ST. TERESA BENEDICTA OF THE CROSS, VIRGIN AND MARTYR •

*Did a people ever hear the voice of God speaking from the
midst of fire, as you did, and live?*
—DEUTERONOMY 4:33

What does it say about us that we seek God?
Shouldn't we be fearful of the power and majesty of
the one we pursue? Since we have confidence that
God is love, we believe that mercy awaits us even in
the midst of fire. Our desire for true communion
says a lot about us, but it says even more about God.

Deuteronomy 4:32–40
Psalm 77:12–13,14–15,16 and 21
Matthew 16:24–28

⇒ 251 ⇐

AUGUST 10

• ST. LAWRENCE, DEACON AND MARTYR •

Well for the man who is gracious and lends,
who conducts his affairs with justice;
He shall never be moved;
the just one shall be in everlasting remembrance.
—PSALM 112:5–6

When St. Lawrence was serving as a deacon in Rome, local authorities demanded that he hand over the Church's riches. Three days later, St. Lawrence brought forward the poor, the widows, and the orphans and announced, "Behold the treasure of the Church." Indeed, our treasure is one another. The glory of the Church is found in how we care for one another, especially the neediest among us.

2 Corinthians 9:6–10
Psalm 112:1–2,5–6,7–8,9
John 12:24–26

Sunday

AUGUST 11

• NINETEENTH SUNDAY IN ORDINARY TIME •

"Much will be required of the person entrusted with much, and still more will be demanded of the person entrusted with more."
—LUKE 12:48

What if we thought about our gifts not as rewards but as responsibilities? Every person is meant to further the mission of love and justice, and we are each given a particular tool kit with which to do so. A talent or passion is not a reward for our goodness but a tool to be put in service of the greater good. What are some ways you might serve others and spread love through the use of your talents today?

Wisdom 18:6–9
Psalm 33:1,12,18–19,20–22 (12b)
Hebrews 11:1–2,8–19 or 11:1–2,8–12
Luke 12:32–48 or 12:35–40

⇒ 253 ⇐

AUGUST 12

• ST. JANE FRANCES DE CHANTAL, RELIGIOUS •

The LORD, your God, shall you fear,
and him shall you serve;
hold fast to him and swear by his name.
—DEUTERONOMY 10:20

St. Jane Frances de Chantal founded the Congregation of the Visitation and accepted women who were rejected by other convents and congregations. The saint we remember today wrote, "Cordial love of the neighbor does not consist in feeling. This love flows not from a heart of flesh but from the heart of our will." I give thanks for all those women who accept and love me without regard for my limits. I remember that such extraordinary love is my vocation, too.

Deuteronomy 10:12–22
Psalm 147:12–13,14–15,19–20
Matthew 17:22–27

AUGUST 13

• SS. PONTIAN, POPE, AND HIPPOLYTUS, PRIEST, MARTYRS •

Think back on the days of old,
reflect on the years of age upon age.
Ask your father and he will inform you,
ask your elders and they will tell you.
—DEUTERONOMY 32:7

I was really loud and outspoken in high school,
qualities that are rarely valued in teenagers. Because
so many people expressed annoyance with me (often
with justification), I internalized the idea that I was
"bad" and all the quieter students were "good." Only
recently, decades later, did I think back over my time
in high school and recognize that I wasn't morally
flawed; I was just loud. Our experiences, both recent
and from times long past, have the power to teach
and change us if we look back with an inner vision
ready to truly see.

Deuteronomy 31:1–8
Deuteronomy 32:3–4ab,7,8,9 and 12
Matthew 18:1–5,10,12–14

Shout joyfully to God, all the earth;
sing praise to the glory of his name.
—PSALM 66:2

St. Maximilian Kolbe writes, "The most deadly poison of our times is indifference. And this happens, although the praise of God should know no limits. Let us strive, therefore, to praise Him to the greatest extent of our powers."

St. Maximilian experienced the cruelty of indifference firsthand as a prisoner at Auschwitz. When ten prisoners escaped from the camp, an officer chosen ten prisoners to starve to death in a bunker as punishment. When one man who was chosen cried out, St. Maximilian offered to take his place. He spent his last two weeks consoling the dying next to him and leading them in prayer—a model of praise and devotion in the face of death and despair. May prayer lead us to deep devotion and heroic service as it did for this great saint.

Deuteronomy 34:1–12
Psalm 66:1–3a,5 and 8,16–17
Matthew 18:15–20

AUGUST 15

• THE ASSUMPTION OF THE BLESSED VIRGIN MARY •

"Blessed are you who believed that what was spoken to you by the Lord would be fulfilled."
—LUKE 1:45

I'd love to know more about Mary, whose bodily assumption into heaven we remember today. What little we know of her radical faith and assent to God's plan is so extraordinary that it changed the course of history. She had no credentials, accomplishments, or renown—none of the things we might think are required to put your faith into action. Her *yes*, so small, was big enough to encompass all of creation.

VIGIL:
1 Chronicles 15:3–4,15–16; 16:1–2
Psalm 132:6–7,9–10,13–14
1 Corinthians 15:54b–57
Luke 11:27–28

DAY:
Revelation 11:19a,12:1–6a,10ab
Psalm 45:10,11,12,16
1 Corinthians 15:20–27
Luke 1:39–56

Give thanks to the LORD, for he is good,
for his mercy endures forever.
—PSALM 136:1

In his 2014 Ash Wednesday homily, Pope Francis
said, "In the face of so many wounds that hurt us and
could harden our hearts, we are called to dive into
the sea of prayer, which is the sea of God's boundless
love, to taste his tenderness." In the face of any
suffering or hurts you may be experiencing, what
kind of tenderness can you find today when you dive
into God's deep sea of love?

Joshua 24:1–13
Psalm 136:1–3,16–18,21–22 and 24
Matthew 19:3–12

AUGUST 17

You will show me the path to life,
fullness of joys in your presence,
the delights at your right hand forever.
—PSALM 16:11

When I was a child, I loved to play in the woods. I realize
now what a special blessing it was to have swaths of
undeveloped land nearby. Each trip into the woods was
an adventure and a chance to find paths through untamed
space. Sometimes I'd follow subtle trails, lightly trod by
those who came before. Some choices were made for me
by nature, when a fallen tree or massive puddle blocked
my path. And sometimes I was led by beauty and delight,
following my intuition in pursuit of lovely things to see,
smell, and feel. There are just as many ways to be led
along the path of life, allowing God's many gifts to steer
us toward the fullness of joy and delight.

Joshua 24:14–29
Psalm 16:1–2a and 5,7–8,11
Matthew 19:13–15

For the sake of the joy that lay before him he endured the cross, despising its shame, and has taken his seat at the right of the throne of God.
—HEBREWS 12:2

There are always opportunities to take the easy way out. We may be tempted to ignore the person whose deep need for attention is grating, to tell a white lie so as to avoid an uncomfortable situation, or to retreat into the safe isolation that demands nothing of us. What keeps you from escaping and helps you stay present? Let us ask for God's grace today to help us remain steadfast.

Jeremiah 38:4–6,8–10
Psalm 40:2,3,4,18 (14b)
Hebrews 12:1–4
Luke 12:49–53

Monday

AUGUST 19

• ST. JOHN EUDES, PRIEST •

*A young man approached Jesus and said, "Teacher, what good must
I do to gain eternal life?"*
—MATTHEW 19:16

The young man goes to Jesus and asks to be taught.
What question is burning in your heart today that you
need to ask the Teacher? What do you think the
Teacher's answer would be?

Judges 2:11–19
Psalm 106:34–35,36–37,39–40,43ab and 44
Matthew 19:16–22

≥ 261 ≤

AUGUST 20

• ST. BERNARD, ABBOT AND DOCTOR OF THE CHURCH •

The LORD himself will give his benefits;
our land shall yield its increase.
—PSALM 85:13

In his book *On Loving God*, St. Bernard of Clairvaux
writes of God's love, "This divine love is true love,
for it is the love of one who wants nothing for
himself." Knowing how rarely love has come close to
such perfection in my own heart, I am in awe of this
pure, selfless love.

Judges 6:11–24a
Psalm 85:9,11–12,13–14
Matthew 19:23–30

AUGUST 21

• ST. PIUS X, POPE •

*"'Take what is yours and go. What if I wish to give this last
one the same as you? Or am I not free to do as I wish with my
own money? Are you envious because I am generous?' Thus,
the last will be first, and the first will be last."*
—MATTHEW 20:14–16

It is easy to recognize the ugliness of envy in others,
less so to root it out in myself. My instinct is to solve
the problem by not paying attention to the things
that trigger my envy. How much better it would be
if I did not ignore but truly rejoiced in the blessings
of others.

Judges 9:6–15
Psalm 21:2–3,4–5,6–7
Matthew 20:1–16

Here I am, Lord;
I come to do your will.
—PSALM 40:8–9

My mother is one of the most thoughtful people
I know, and this quality comes from her habit of
paying attention. If she hears someone talking about
liking a particular candy bar, she will pick one up for
him or her the next time she's at a store. If she
notices a young niece's or nephew's interest in an
action hero or cartoon character, that character will
be on the front of the next birthday card she sends.
Her example reminds me to be observant of the
needs of the world, both large and small.
Opportunities to do God's will appear when we
pay attention.

Judges 11:29–39a
Psalm 40:5,7–8a,8b–9,10
Matthew 22:1–14

Friday

AUGUST 23

• ST. ROSE OF LIMA, VIRGIN •

*"The whole law and the prophets depend on these two
commandments."*
—MATTHEW 22:40

Love of God and love of neighbor: everything
depends on these. Love should guide our decisions.
It is our eternal lodestar.

Ruth 1:1,3–6,14b–16,22
Psalm 146:5–6ab,6c–7,8–9a,9bc–10
Matthew 22:34–40

Your Kingdom is a Kingdom for all ages,
and your dominion endures through all generations.
—PSALM 145:13

The kingdom of God is mentioned throughout
Scripture. Jesus tells us that the kingdom is at hand.
The kingdom is among us. We may not understand
this fully during our lives, but we can work for a
world in which it is apparent that God's law of love
reigns supreme.

Revelation 21:9b–14
Psalm 145:10–11,12–13,17–18
John 1:45–51

Sunday
August 25

For steadfast is his kindness toward us,
and the fidelity of the LORD endures forever.
—PSALM 117:2

We belong to God, who will be faithful to us for all
ages. Let the knowledge of this faithfulness give you
comfort and confidence today. You are a precious
child of God. You are beloved. And this love
endures forever.

Isaiah 66:18–21
Psalm 117:1,2
Hebrews 12:5–7,11–13
Luke 13:22–30

For our Gospel did not come to you in word alone, but also in power and in the Holy Spirit and with much conviction. You know what sort of people we were among you for your sake.
—1 THESSALONIANS 1:5

Faith is more than a collection of beliefs. The Good News does not merely satisfy our intellect. It transforms us completely, in every part of our lives. Jesus' life, death, and Resurrection give us a model of how to love radically and how to stay true to ourselves even in the face of great danger. We take the stories from the page and out into the world. How can you bring the gospel to life today?

1 Thessalonians 1:1–5,8b–10
Psalm 149:1b–2,3–4,5–6a and 9b
Matthew 23:13–22

With such affection for you, we were determined to share with you not only the Gospel of God, but our very selves as well, so dearly beloved had you become to us.
—1 THESSALONIANS 2:8

St. Monica, the mother of St. Augustine, wanted her son to accept the Good News because of her deep love for him. She steadfastly prayed and worked for his conversion. From her example, we know that our efforts at evangelization cannot only be a transferral of information. They must include a sharing of our very selves. For sharing the gospel should always be rooted in love.

1 Thessalonians 2:1–8
Psalm 139:1–3,4–6
Matthew 23:23–26

AUGUST 28

• ST. AUGUSTINE, BISHOP AND DOCTOR OF THE CHURCH •

Where can I go from your spirit?
From your presence where can I flee?
—PSALM 139:7

In Book X of *Confessions*, St. Augustine writes to the
Lord, "Lo, you were within, but I outside, seeking
there for you. . . . You were with me but I was not
with you." Many of us have probably experienced
the same—looking for God outside of ourselves,
relying on others or outside stimuli. But we know
that God is inside, waiting patiently. There is
nowhere we can go that God will not be with us.
How have you experienced the patience of God?

1 Thessalonians 2:9–13
Psalm 139:7–8,9–10,11–12ab
Matthew 23:27–32

Thursday

AUGUST 29

• THE PASSION OF ST. JOHN THE BAPTIST •

Return, O LORD! How long?
Have pity on your servants!
—PSALM 90:13

If Jesus walked into the room right now, would you be ready to meet him? Maybe you have an unhealthy habit you want to shake first, a grudge you should resolve, or a distraction with which you need to make peace. What changes can you make that will help you be ready to meet Jesus whenever he may appear?

1 Thessalonians 3:7–13
Psalm 90:3–5a,12–13,14 and 17
Mark 6:17–29

AUGUST 30

Light dawns for the just;
and gladness, for the upright of heart.
—PSALM 97:11

Living uprightly is a surer path to happiness than
any scheme or machination. No matter what befalls,
we know we have done what we ought.

1 Thessalonians 4:1–8
Psalm 97:1 and 2b,5–6,10,11–12
Matthew 25:1–13

AUGUST 31

Nevertheless we urge you, brothers and sisters, to progress even more, and to aspire to live a tranquil life, to mind your own affairs, and to work with your own hands, as we instructed you.
—1 THESSALONIANS 4:10–11

Paul's advice is timeless: live peacefully and do an honest day's work. Don't worry about others' business, and love one another. When living such a life feels like a struggle, I am tempted to blame my environment. I imagine I could live peacefully if other people were different, if life weren't busy, if current events didn't feel so threatening. Paul's deep relationship with the living Christ gave him confidence, courage, and peace in the midst of troubles. I seek that same relationship.

1 Thessalonians 4:9–11
Psalm 98:1,7–8,9
Matthew 25:14–30

SEPTEMBER 1

• TWENTY-SECOND SUNDAY IN ORDINARY TIME •

My child, conduct your affairs with humility,
and you will be loved more than a giver of gifts.
—SIRACH 3:17

The world does not revolve around me. This simple lesson, which parents try so hard to impart to children, still needs to be learned and relearned in adulthood. I find that when I shift my focus to others, I am quickly reminded that each person has as rich an interior life as I do, that they struggle and rejoice and are as fully human as I am. By truly listening to and valuing them, I demonstrate some of the humility that Scripture encourages.

Sirach 3:17–18,20,28–29
Psalm 68:4–5,6–7,10–11
Hebrews 12:18–19,22–24a
Luke 14:1,7–14

SEPTEMBER 2

*Then we who are alive, who are left, will be caught up together
with them in the clouds to meet the Lord in the air. Thus we
shall always be with the Lord. Therefore, console one another
with these words.*

—1 THESSALONIANS 4:17–18

During dark times, we can turn to the word of God
for consolation and hope. Perhaps you are like me
and find musical settings of Scripture to be
especially comforting. Certain pieces, like Jeanne
Cotter's setting of Psalm 103 and the Taizé mantras
"My Peace" and "Nada Te Turbe," have imprinted
themselves on my heart and come to mind unbidden
when I need them. What are the passages or songs
to which you turn?

1 Thessalonians 4:13–18
Psalm 96:1 and 3,4–5,11–12,13
Luke 4:16–30

Tuesday

SEPTEMBER 3

• ST. GREGORY THE GREAT, POPE AND DOCTOR OF THE CHURCH •

For all of you are children of the light and children of the day.
We are not of the night or of darkness.
—1 THESSALONIANS 5:5

Light allows us to see. We can see beauty and
goodness with gratitude and know that they are of
God. We can see confusion and complexity without
fear, knowing that the light of Christ is our guide.
And we can see tragedy and evil with compassion,
knowing that God's illuminating love always has the
final word.

1 Thessalonians 5:1–6,9–11
Psalm 27:1,4,13–14
Luke 4:31–37

⇉ 276 ⇇

SEPTEMBER 4

I, like a green olive tree
in the house of God,
Trust in the mercy of God
forever and ever.
—PSALM 52:10

I planted a lavender plant in front of our
triple-decker that surprised me by growing. Its
fragrant stalks keep reaching up and bearing the
occasional flower, unperturbed by what goes on
around it. There was an entire summer of workers
jackhammering on the sidewalk, lines of traffic
during rush hour, and parades of pedestrians that
noisily pass down our urban street. But still it grows,
because that's what it was made to do. Let us strive
to be so confident and single-minded in our growth.

Colossians 1:1–8
Psalm 52:10,11
Luke 4:38–44

SEPTEMBER 5

*Simon said in reply, "Master, we have worked hard all night
and have caught nothing, but at your command I will
lower the nets."*
—LUKE 5:5

In today's reading, we witness Simon put his net in
the water, perhaps with a surreptitious eye roll at the
preacher's request. But then the nets are full, the boat
gets full, and the fisherman's heart is full of wonder
at this miracle. He and his companions leave
everything to follow Jesus because of this sign—a
sign that was made possible by Simon's willingness
to try something despite his doubts.

Colossians 1:9–14
Psalm 98:2–3ab,3cd–4,5–6
Luke 5:1–11

Come with joy into the presence of the Lord.
—PSALM 100:2

In his book *The Joy of the Gospel*, Pope Francis writes, "Joy adapts and changes, but it always endures, even as a flicker of light born of our personal certainty that, when everything is said and done, we are infinitely loved." What brought you joy today?

Colossians 1:15–20
Psalm 100:1b–2,3,4,5
Luke 5:33–39

Saturday

SEPTEMBER 7

Freely will I offer you sacrifice;
I will praise your name, O LORD, for its goodness.
—PSALM 54:8

May my words today express the love of God that
lives in my heart. Too often it feels more satisfying
to use my words for gossip, cattiness, or criticism. I
seek the peace, wisdom, and understanding that help
me to see that praise is more suitable—and more
deeply satisfying.

Colossians 1:21–23
Psalm 54:3–4,6 and 8
Luke 6:1–5

SEPTEMBER 8

• TWENTY-THIRD SUNDAY IN ORDINARY TIME •

And may the gracious care of the LORD our God be ours;
prosper the work of our hands for us!
Prosper the work of our hands!
—PSALM 90:17

The work of our hands can be found in our families
and friendships, our jobs, our creative pursuits.
Philanthropy. Volunteering. Gardening. Laundry.
We pray that God's gracious care will prosper the
work of our hands.

Wisdom 9:13–18b
Psalm 90:3–4,5–6,12–13,14,17 (1)
Philemon 9–10,12–17
Luke 14:25–33

*It is he whom we proclaim, admonishing everyone and
teaching everyone with all wisdom, that we may present
everyone perfect in Christ.*
—COLOSSIANS 1:28

St. Peter Claver served slaves in Colombia for
decades. He fed them and tended to their bodily
needs, believing that "we must speak to them with
our hands before we speak to them with our lips."
He then told them of Christ and did the same with
the slave owners in his ongoing efforts to convince
them to change their cruel behavior. His Christlike
care proclaimed Christ's love.

Colossians 1:24–2:3
Psalm 62:6–7,9
Luke 6:6–11

SEPTEMBER 10

*Jesus departed to the mountain to pray, and he spent the night
in prayer to God.*
—LUKE 6:12

There is a hermitage on the top of Mount Subasio in
Assisi, Italy, to which St. Francis of Assisi used to
escape to pray. The paths are marked with signs
requesting "Silenzio," and the shady wooden paths
lead to several simple grottos. When I visited the
hermitage, we walked up the quiet, winding miles
from the town and found both rest and peace on the
simple benches that dot its quiet expanse. Each
reminder of God's holy presence drew me deeper
into the profundity of this mini-pilgrimage. What
would our lives be like if every path were lined with
stops for prayer?

Colossians 2:6–15
Psalm 145:1b–2,8–9,10–11
Luke 6:12–19

SEPTEMBER 11

But now you must put them all away: anger, fury, malice,
slander, and obscene language out of your mouths.
—COLOSSIANS 3:8

I've never been comfortable with the expression
"have a temper," as it makes an asset out of what is
really a deficiency: a lack of self-control. Moving
beyond anger and fury is within my control. Just as I
may have cycles of building frustration, when one
irritant leads me to be increasingly annoyed with
other things, I have also discovered cycles of
tranquility, when one moment of choosing a positive
response makes me increasingly content. It is a long
path to the peace that Christ wants for us, and he
invites us, through our free will, to participate in
that journey.

Colossians 3:1–11
Psalm 145:2–3,10–11,12–13ab
Luke 6:20–26

SEPTEMBER 12

Let the word of Christ dwell in you richly, as in all wisdom
you teach and admonish one another, singing psalms, hymns,
and spiritual songs with gratitude in your hearts to God.
—COLOSSIANS 3:16

The word of Christ can dwell in me only if I am
exposed to it. Time spent with Scripture and holy
writing can transform my heart. I savor Christ's
words. How do you experience and savor
Christ's words?

Colossians 3:12–17
Psalm 150:1b–2,3–4,5–6
Luke 6:27–38

⇒ 285 ⇐

*Indeed, the grace of our Lord has been abundant, along with
the faith and love that are in Christ Jesus.*
—1 TIMOTHY 1:14

St. John Chrysostom died in exile in 407. In the
book *The Fathers*, Pope Benedict writes about
St. John's faithful belief in God's loving plan: "Even if
we are unable to unravel the details of our personal
and collective history, we know that God's plan is
always inspired by his love. Thus, despite his
suffering, Chrysostom reaffirmed the discovery that
God loves each one of us with an infinite love and
therefore desires salvation for us all."

1 Timothy 1:1–2,12–14
Psalm 16:1b–2a and 5,7–8,11
Luke 6:39–42

SEPTEMBER 14

• THE EXALTATION OF THE HOLY CROSS •

For God did not send his Son into the world to condemn the world, but that the world might be saved through him.
—JOHN 3:17

God chose a particular time for the Son to enter the world and a particular time for the cross to become the unlikely vehicle for our salvation. He showed us that terror and brutality are always conquered by love and life.

Numbers 21:4b–9
Psalm 78:1bc–2,34–35,36–37,38
Philippians 2:6–11
John 3:13–17

SEPTEMBER 15

• TWENTY-FOURTH SUNDAY IN ORDINARY TIME •

"'Take the fattened calf and slaughter it. Then let us celebrate with a feast, because this son of mine was dead, and has come back to life again; he was lost, and has been found.' Then the celebration began."
—LUKE 15:23–24

The son who has squandered his inheritance tells his father, "I no longer deserve to be called your son," but his father pays no mind. We are all children of God, and no sin or absence can change that.

Exodus 32:7–11,13–14
Psalm 51:3–4,12–13,17,19
1 Timothy 1:12–17
Luke 15:1–32 or 15:1–10

Beloved: First of all, I ask that supplications, prayers, petitions, and thanksgivings be offered for everyone, for kings and for all in authority, that we may lead a quiet and tranquil life in all devotion and dignity.

—1 TIMOTHY 2:1–2

May all those in authority—including ourselves—use that authority to allow, as Paul's letter to Timothy states, a "quiet and tranquil life in all devotion and dignity." When we recognize this as a true goal of leadership, how does that change our efforts?

1 Timothy 2:1–8
Psalm 28:2,7,8–9
Luke 7:1–10

I will persevere in the way of integrity;
when will you come to me?
—PSALM 101:2

Integrity derives from *integer*, meaning "whole" in
Latin. If you consider your life from a bird's-eye
view, do you see consistency in your behavior, or are
there areas where your fundamental morals go on
the back burner? Turn your attention to those
inconsistent spots. Can you make changes that will
help you become more whole?

1 Timothy 3:1–13
Psalm 101:1b–2ab,2cd–3ab,5,6
Luke 7:11–17

⇒ 290 ⇐

SEPTEMBER 18

*"They are like children who sit in the marketplace and call to
one another,
'We played the flute for you, but you did not dance.
We sang a dirge, but you did not weep.'"*
—LUKE 7:32

Is God enough for you? We get so caught up in our
presuppositions and needs that we risk putting our
own demands on the Lord. Love and grace
are enough.

1 Timothy 3:14–16
Psalm 111:1–2,3–4,5–6
Luke 7:31–35

SEPTEMBER 19

Beloved: Let no one have contempt for your youth, but set an example for those who believe, in speech, conduct, love, faith, and purity.

—1 TIMOTHY 4:12

I work with young men just entering their teen years who have often been told that the momentous decisions they will make about their lives won't happen until high school, college, or beyond. In my experience, however, the biggest decisions about what kind of person they want to be are made in these early years. We sell young people short when we fail to recognize the vibrant inner lives of children and their efforts to be Christlike. It is never too early for someone to be an example of virtue.

1 Timothy 4:12–16
Psalm 111:7–8,9,10
Luke 7:36–50

Friday

SEPTEMBER 20

Why should I fear in evil days
when my wicked ensnarers ring me round?
—PSALM 49:6

We only know a few names of the Korean martyrs
commemorated today, though we do know their
leaders and their suffering. St. Andrew Kim Tae-gŏn
and St. Paul Chŏng Ha-sang were persecuted for
their missionary work in seventeenth-century Korea.
St. Andrew was arrested and beheaded near Seoul,
and many others who were later beatified were
brutally murdered. While many of their lives are
unknown, we do know that their suffering drew
them close to the heart of God.

1 Timothy 6:2c–12
Psalm 49:6–7,8–10,17–18,19–20
Luke 8:1–3

Saturday

SEPTEMBER 21

• ST. MATTHEW, APOSTLE AND EVANGELIST •

*Day pours out the word to day,
and night to night imparts knowledge.*
—PSALM 19:3

The artist Caravaggio depicted many scenes from
the life of St. Matthew. Some of them are intimate:
The Inspiration of St. Matthew and *St. Matthew and the
Angel* show the aged evangelist with just his writing
tools and a guiding angel. Some are crowded with
people, such as the chaotic *The Martyrdom of
St. Matthew* and *The Calling of St. Matthew,* in which
Jesus' illuminated hand cuts through the crowd with
a gesture of beckoning. I find Caravaggio's signature
technique of combining light and shadow to be both
captivating and instructive. Light and darkness live
side by side, and through each God is working.

Ephesians 4:1–7,11–13
Psalm 19:2–3,4–5
Matthew 9:9–13

*"The person who is trustworthy in very small matters is also
trustworthy in great ones; and the person who is dishonest in
very small matters is also dishonest in great ones."*
—LUKE 16:10

Many years ago, my family suddenly lost two
members. I saw firsthand true strength and
perseverance through crushing grief, and I came to
understand this truth: crisis does not shape character
but rather it reveals it. We were able to endure
because we had already trained ourselves in love.
From that time forward, I committed myself to
cultivating prayerfulness and faith when times were
easy so that I could remain graceful and loving when
times were difficult.

Amos 8:4–7
Psalm 113:1–2,4–6,7–8
1 Timothy 2:1–8
Luke 16:1–13 or 16:10–13

SEPTEMBER 23

The LORD has done marvels for us.
—PSALM 126:3

An oft-quoted saying of Padre Pio, the beloved Italian mystic and friar, is "Pray, hope, and don't worry." Which of these three challenges you the most?

Ezra 1:1–6
Psalm 126:1b–2ab,2cd–3,4–5,6
Luke 8:16–18

SEPTEMBER 24

The children of Israel—priests, Levites, and the other returned exiles—celebrated the dedication of this house of God with joy.
—EZRA 6:16

In today's reading from Ezra, the Jews rejoiced when they finally finished rebuilding the temple. Consider the things in life that you have built, such as a career, family, education, or hobbies. How have you ensured that they are built for the greater glory of God?

Ezra 6:7–8,12b,14–20
Psalm 122:1–2,3–4ab,4cd–5
Luke 8:19–21

SEPTEMBER 25

Then they set out and went from village to village proclaiming
the good news and curing diseases everywhere.
—LUKE 9:6

When the Twelve proclaim the Good News on their
travels, they do so not only with words but also with
acts that show Jesus' healing power. The Gospels
give us few details of their ministry during Jesus' life,
but Acts of the Apostles is filled with the bold
proclamations of Jesus' first followers, beginning
with Peter's prophetic exhortation at Pentecost.
Later, we see Peter healing a bedridden man, raising
Tabitha to life, and breaking custom to dine with
Cornelius, a God-fearing Gentile. The Good News
is not just a set of teachings to repeat but a mission
of healing and inclusion that we, like the apostles,
can emulate.

Ezra 9:5–9
Tobit 13:2,3–4a,4befghn,7–8
Luke 9:1–6

SEPTEMBER 26

Let them praise his name in the festive dance,
let them sing praise to him with timbrel and harp.
—PSALM 149:3

Let the love of God infect you, changing your entire
body and soul. Which of your joys and blessings are
so great that you cannot help but proclaim praise?

Haggai 1:1–8
Psalm 149:1b–2,3–4,5–6a and 9b
Luke 9:7–9

Send forth your light and your fidelity;
they shall lead me on
And bring me to your holy mountain,
to your dwelling-place.
—PSALM 43:3

My first exposure to St. Vincent de Paul was through the St. Vincent de Paul Society. The parish of my youth filled a truck once a month with grocery bags of donations. The Society delivered furniture and hosted coffee and donuts. In my mind's eye, I can see the men and women greeting parishioners by name as they loaded our donations into the back of the truck. I am so grateful for their example of charity, which begins with kindness and relationship.

Haggai 2:1–9
Psalm 43:1,2,3,4
Luke 9:18–22

SEPTEMBER 28

• ST. WENCESLAUS, MARTYR • ST. LAWRENCE RUIZ AND
COMPANIONS, MARTYRS •

Then the virgins shall make merry and dance,
and young men and old as well.
I will turn their mourning into joy.
I will console and gladden them after their sorrows.
—JEREMIAH 31:13

The Bohemian Duke Wenceslaus was betrayed by
his brother due to political rivalry, and he was killed
by his brother's supporters on the way to Mass. He
was known for his Christian faith and leadership and
for the charitable spirit described in the hymn
"Good King Wenceslaus," which concludes, "Ye who
now will bless the poor / shall yourselves find
blessing."

Zechariah 2:5–9,14–15a
Jeremiah 31:10,11–12ab,13
Luke 9:43b–45

SEPTEMBER 29

*But you, man of God, pursue righteousness, devotion, faith,
love, patience, and gentleness.*
—1 TIMOTHY 6:11

Since I work at an all-boys school, I pay close
attention to the models of masculinity presented in
popular culture. Movies depict men as sexually
reckless and aggressive, advertisers encourage men
and boys to be "tough" by driving big cars and
purchasing expensive gear, and many television
series present emotionally stunted men as both the
norm and a punchline. One antidote to these poor
examples is the instruction Paul gave to Timothy:
Let us all, men and women, "pursue righteousness,
devotion, faith, love, patience, and gentleness."

Amos 6:1a, 4–7
Psalm 146:7,8–9,9–10 (1b)
1 Timothy 6:11–16
Luke 16:19–31

An argument arose among the disciples about which of them
was the greatest.
—LUKE 9:46

Even those closest to Jesus engaged in prideful squabbling. In today's reading from Luke, the apostles argue about which one of them is the greatest. Jesus responds by placing a child by his side and saying, "Whoever receives this child in my name receives me, and whoever receives me receives the one who sent me. For the one who is least among all of you is the one who is the greatest" (Luke 9:48). When we are tempted to bicker, can we let Jesus into our hearts and put our pride aside?

Zechariah 8:1–8
Psalm 102:16–18,19–21,29 and 22–23
Luke 9:46–50

OCTOBER 1

• ST. THÉRÈSE OF THE CHILD JESUS, VIRGIN AND DOCTOR OF
THE CHURCH •

*Many peoples and strong nations shall come to seek the LORD
of hosts in Jerusalem and to implore the favor of the LORD.*
—ZECHARIAH 8:22

We come to God in moments of seeking, as
St. Thérèse of Lisieux describes in *Story of a Soul*. She
writes, "Prayer is, for me, an outburst from the heart;
it is a simple glance darted upwards to Heaven; it is a
cry of gratitude and of love in the midst of trial as in
the midst of joy!"

Zechariah 8:20–23
Psalm 87:1b–3,4–5,6–7
Luke 9:51–56

Wednesday

OCTOBER 2

• THE HOLY GUARDIAN ANGELS •

Let my tongue be silenced if I ever forget you!
—PSALM 137:6

I often forget what is most important because I let other things crowd my heart. I give in to the smug satisfaction of anger or focus so far inward that selfishness overtakes me. When I keep God's love at the center, I don't need to set myself above others—I'm moved to treat all as the beloved children of God that they are. Then I can use my words and hands in true service.

Nehemiah 2:1–8
Psalm 137:1–2,3,4–5,6
Matthew 18:1–5,10

OCTOBER 3

He said to them, "The harvest is abundant but the laborers are few; so ask the master of the harvest to send out laborers for his harvest."
—LUKE 10:2

In his poem "Hurrahing in Harvest," the Jesuit poet Gerard Manley Hopkins describes the end of summer as "barbarous in beauty." Look for wild beauty today and consider how God is inviting you to participate in the cultivation of the world's lavish loveliness.

Nehemiah 8:1–4a,5–6,7b–12
Psalm 19:8,9,10,11
Luke 10:1–12

Friday

OCTOBER 4

• ST. FRANCIS OF ASSISI •

Remember not against us the iniquities of the past;
may your compassion quickly come to us,
for we are brought very low.
—PSALM 79:8

St. Francis of Assisi repented of the sins of his youth
and then got to work building something better. His
embrace of simplicity did not lead to asceticism for
its own sake but to a radical freedom that
revolutionized the Church and society. On his feast
day, pray for the freedom that Francis
put into service.

Baruch 1:15–22
Psalm 79:1b–2,3–5,8,9
Luke 10:13–16

Turning to the disciples in private he said, "Blessed are the eyes that see what you see."
—LUKE 10:23

Faith is a gift that we are blessed to receive. We know that it is also an effort. We strive to do that which St. Ignatius prayed for: to see more clearly, love more dearly, and follow more nearly. In his book *Reaching Out*, Henri Nouwen writes, "The paradox of prayer is that we have to learn how to pray while we can only receive it as a gift. We cannot plan, organize or manipulate God, but without a careful discipleship we cannot receive him either."

Baruch 4:5–12,27–29
Psalm 69:33–35,36–37
Luke 10:17–24

*"When you have done all you have been commanded, say,
'We are unprofitable servants; we have done what we were
obliged to do.'"*
—LUKE 17:10

This Gospel passage reminds me to keep my head
down and do the right thing. God's desires for me
are enough to keep me busy for a lifetime. Doing
what I was made for—what all of us were made
for—loving, creating, and serving—doesn't earn
gold stars. The best thing we have is God's love,
which cannot be earned.

Habakkuk 1:2–3,2:2–4
Psalm 95:1–2,6–7,8–9 (8)
2 Timothy 1:6–8,13–14
Luke 17:5–10

"But a Samaritan traveler who came upon him was moved with compassion at the sight."
—LUKE 10:33

When your heart is moved toward someone, act on it quickly, before fear or distraction prevent you from acting as the Samaritan did.

Jonah 1:1–2:2,11
Jonah 2:3,4,5,8
Luke 10:25–37

If you, O LORD, mark iniquities,
LORD, who can stand?
But with you is forgiveness,
that you may be revered.
—PSALM 130:3–4

May I never cease to marvel at the mercy of the
Lord, which does not count my failings but forgives.
When I need forgiveness, I push myself to admit my
fault to whomever I have hurt. I've found that this
becomes easier the more I do it. Hiding or denying
my sinfulness does not add anything to my value,
and acknowledging my failings helps me to make
amends. The Lord's mercy is wide enough for
any sin.

Jonah 3:1–10
Psalm 130:1b–2,3–4ab,7–8
Luke 10:38–42

OCTOBER 9

• ST. DENIS, BISHOP, AND COMPANIONS, MARTYRS •
ST. JOHN LEONARDI, PRIEST •

*Jesus was praying in a certain place, and when he had
finished, one of his disciples said to him, "Lord, teach us to
pray just as John taught his disciples."*

—LUKE 11:1

Whenever I have asked God to teach me to pray, I
have felt foolish, thinking, *Shouldn't I know how to do
this?* But saying "Lord, teach me to pray" is a prayer
in itself.

Jonah 4:1–11
Psalm 86:3–4,5–6,9–10
Luke 11:1–4

OCTOBER 10

"I tell you, if he does not get up to give him the loaves because of their friendship, he will get up to give him whatever he needs because of his persistence."
—LUKE 11:8

Do not give up on bringing your needs to God, who wants to hear from you. Our need may be the most vulnerable thing about us, that which we hide because it is too wide a window into the broken parts of our souls. If you have a deep longing, share it with the One who desires to be our closest friend.

Malachi 3:13–20b
Psalm 1:1–2,3,4 and 6
Luke 11:5–13

The Lord will judge the world with justice.
—PSALM 9:9

Jesus proclaimed that his return would come with
judgment. But this judgment will be rooted in
justice, just as the gospel is. When we are uncertain
of what is just, we can turn to the Good News
for guidance.

Joel 1:13–15,2:1–2
Psalm 9:2–3,6 and 16,8–9
Luke 11:15–26

OCTOBER 12

*He replied, "Rather, blessed are those who hear the word of
God and observe it."*
—LUKE 11:28

How is God speaking to you today? Through
Scripture or private prayer? Through friends or
family? Each day comes with a new opportunity to
hear the word of God and observe it.

Joel 4:12–21
Psalm 97:1–2,5–6,11–12
Luke 11:27–28

⋑ 315 ⋐

But the word of God is not chained.

—2 TIMOTHY 2:9

No matter the limits of our bodies, we are part of a
love that is limitless.

2 Kings 5:14–17
Psalm 98:1,2–3,3–4
2 Timothy 2:8–13
Luke 17:11–19

OCTOBER 14

• ST. CALLISTUS I, POPE AND MARTYR •

Grace to you and peace from God our Father and the Lord Jesus Christ.
—ROMANS 1:7

As I move through my day, I hope to offer grace and peace to all whom I encounter. And when I fail, as I inevitably will, I stop and reset and try again.

Romans 1:1–7
Psalm 98:1,2–3ab,3cd–4
Luke 11:29–32

OCTOBER 15

• ST. TERESA OF JESUS, VIRGIN AND DOCTOR OF THE CHURCH •

Brothers and sisters: I am not ashamed of the Gospel.
—ROMANS 1:16

St. Teresa of Ávila was feisty, sociable, and driven. She followed her inclination to reform religious life despite criticism because she was close to God in prayer. She was honest about her sinfulness and temptations, and she fought them while keeping her high spirits. On her feast day, we remember her merriment in joy. As she says, "May God protect me from gloomy saints."

Romans 1:16–25
Psalm 19:2–3,4–5
Luke 11:37–41

OCTOBER 16

• ST. HEDWIG, RELIGIOUS • ST. MARGARET MARY ALACOQUE, VIRGIN •

Trust in him at all times, O my people!
Pour out your hearts before him;
God is our refuge!
—PSALM 62:9

Jesus revealed his heart, overflowing with love, to
St. Margaret Mary. With the knowledge that he
shares his heart with us, we can unreservedly pour
out our hearts to him.

Romans 2:1–11
Psalm 62:2–3,6–7,9
Luke 11:42–46

My soul waits for the LORD
more than sentinels wait for the dawn.
—PSALM 130:6

With a diabetic in the family, I think a lot about
insulin. When this hormone isn't present or
perceivable, the whole body is affected, prompting
thirst, discomfort, and stress on vital organs. Our
systems were made to need insulin. On a spiritual
level, our souls were made to need God. When my
heart feels empty, I am desperate for the consolation
of the Spirit. It affects my entire system.

Romans 3:21–30
Psalm 130:1b–2,3–4,5–6ab
Luke 11:47–54

OCTOBER 18

• ST. LUKE, EVANGELIST •

Your friends make known, O Lord,
the glorious splendor of your Kingdom.
—PSALM 145:12

One of the simplest definitions of "grace" that I use
in my classroom is "friendship with God." Not a bad
summary of such a rich theological concept. We
have many models of friendship with Jesus, from
those who were there from the beginning, like
St. Luke, to saints through the ages and those in our
lives. Who are your role models of
friendship with God?

2 Timothy 4:10–17b
Psalm 145:10–11,12–13,17–18
Luke 10:1–9

He believed, hoping against hope, that he would become the
father of many nations, *according to what was said,*
Thus shall your descendants be.
—ROMANS 4:18

Abraham put his faith in God's promises, despite
discouraging evidence to the contrary. God's
promise to us is to remain by our side. Have faith.

Romans 4:13,16–18
Psalm 105:6–7,8–9,42–43
Luke 12:8–12

"For a long time the judge was unwilling, but eventually he thought, 'While it is true that I neither fear God nor respect any human being, because this widow keeps bothering me I shall deliver a just decision for her lest she finally come and strike me.'"

—LUKE 18:4–5

When my illness was at its worst, I was in severe pain for almost an entire year. I developed an affinity for the persistent widow during that time, as I beat on the doors of God's house in prayer, begging for relief. I had no magical thinking about "earning" my healing by making a certain number of requests, but I took comfort in the idea that God values my persistence.

Exodus 17:8–13
Psalm 121:1–2,3–4,5–6,7–8
2 Timothy 3:14–4:2
Luke 18:1–8

Then he said to the crowd, "Take care to guard against all greed, for though one may be rich, one's life does not consist of possessions."
—LUKE 12:15

Money is a convenient metric for those who desire superiority: the more you have, the better you are. But we know our value does not come from what we have or from being superior to others. Our value comes from being God's daughters and sons.

Romans 4:20–25
Luke 1:69–70,71–72,73–75
Luke 12:13–21

OCTOBER 22

• ST. JOHN PAUL II, POPE •

Sacrifice or oblation you wished not, / but ears open to obedience you gave me. / Burnt offerings or sin-offerings you sought not; / then said I, "Behold I come."
—PSALM 40:7–8

St. John Paul II offered his eloquence, charisma, and many other talents to God and the Church. His twenty-seven-year pontificate spanned decades of massive technological advances, allowing him to travel far more widely than his predecessors and to be present to the world through video and images. He wrote beautifully, motivating the faithful with his words, and was quick with a quip to inspire laughter and ease. Many images from his papacy are just as instructive as his words: a moment of forgiveness with his would-be assassin, demonstrating radical mercy, and his last years of increasing frailty showing us how to age with grace and to see human value at all stages of life. John Paul II gave himself fully to the Church and the world. And he shows us that any one of us can offer who we are in service of the Lord.

Romans 5:12,15b,17–19,20b–21
Psalm 40:7–8a, 8b–9,10,17
Luke 12:35–38

Freed from sin, you have become slaves of righteousness.
—ROMANS 6:18

I have heard plenty of jokes about Catholic guilt, but in truth there are times I cherish those feelings of guilt. When I sin, my conscience should tell me I have done something wrong. The pit I get in my stomach when I fail to love in word or deed is a sign that my body is becoming a slave to righteousness, even if my heart does not always obey the master. While we do not want to feel consumed by guilt all the time, we can trust that it can be a good harbinger at times.

Romans 6:12–18
Psalm 124:1b–3,4–6,7–8
Luke 12:39–48

OCTOBER 24

Jesus said to his disciples: "I have come to set the earth on fire, and how I wish it were already blazing!"
—LUKE 12:49

The way of discipleship is often treacherous. Do not be fooled into thinking that the path of least resistance is the one that leads to holiness. The way is hard, but the goal is glory.

Romans 6:19–23
Psalm 1:1–2,3,4 and 6
Luke 12:49–53

OCTOBER 25

You are good and bountiful;
teach me your statutes.
—PSALM 119:68

We love and obey God's commandments because we
know the God who gave them to us is good. When
we share this faith with others, do we also share the
love of the Lord? An education in faith that only
focuses on the law and not on the goodness of God
is incomplete.

Romans 7:18–25a
Psalm 119:66,68,76,77,93,94
Luke 12:54–59

⇒ 328 ⇐

*For those who live according to the flesh are concerned with
the things of the flesh, but those who live according to the spirit
with the things of the spirit. The concern of the flesh is death,
but the concern of the spirit is life and peace.*
—ROMANS 8:5–6

If you know what matters to you, don't judge
yourself by other people's priorities. As I have gotten
older, I have become more comfortable ignoring
what is "cool" when considering moral questions. As
today's reading states, may we be more concerned
with things of the spirit, with how the Holy Spirit is
shaping our own spirits.

Romans 8:1–11
Psalm 24:1b–2,3–4ab,5–6
Luke 13:1–9

Sunday

OCTOBER 27

• THIRTIETH SUNDAY IN ORDINARY TIME •

The LORD is a God of justice,
who knows no favorites.
Though not unduly partial toward the weak,
yet he hears the cry of the oppressed.
—SIRACH 35:12–13

Which is more challenging for you: having no
favorites or being attentive to the cry of the poor?
We emulate God when we love all and care for the
vulnerable.

Sirach 35:12–14,16–18
Psalm 34:2–3,17–18,19,23 (7a)
2 Timothy 4:6–8,16–18
Luke 18:9–14

⇒ 330 ⇐

Through him the whole structure is held together and grows into a temple sacred in the Lord; in him you are also being built together into a dwelling place of God in the Spirit.
—EPHESIANS 2:21–22

With many passions and projects pulling me in disparate directions, I often feel like a jumble of parts rather than a coherent whole. When I feel most disjointed, my prayer seeks guidance on what holds the parts together. My obligations and enthusiasm should lead to a fuller life in Christ.

Ephesians 2:19–22
Psalm 19:2–3,4–5
Luke 6:12–16

OCTOBER 29

*Brothers and sisters: I consider that the sufferings of this
present time are as nothing compared with the glory to be
revealed for us.*
—ROMANS 8:18

Suffering is real. Paul's words don't minimize
suffering or promise it will be less painful. But he
predicts that what comes after the suffering will be
infinitely more glorious, which is just what Jesus
showed us on the cross and in the empty tomb.

Romans 8:18–25
Psalm 126:1b–2ab,2cd–3,4–5,6
Luke 13:18–21

Though I trusted in your mercy,
Let my heart rejoice in your salvation;
let me sing of the LORD, "He has been good to me."
—PSALM 13:6

In her book *Walking on Water*, Madeleine L'Engle
writes, "We draw people to Christ not by loudly
discrediting what they believe, by telling them how
wrong they are and how right we are, but by
showing them a light that is so lovely that they want
with all their hearts to know the source of it." Does
your life sing joyfully of God's goodness?

Romans 8:26–30
Psalm 13:4–5,6
Luke 13:22–30

OCTOBER 31

What will separate us from the love of Christ? Will anguish,
or distress, or persecution, or famine, or nakedness, or peril, or
the sword?
—ROMANS 8:35

Paul's deep familiarity with the Hebrew Scripture
made him aware of the long history of God's
unwavering fidelity. Through idolatry and sin,
famine and enslavement, the faithfulness of the Lord
endured. And so it is today: nothing can separate us
from the love of God.

Romans 8:31b–39
Psalm 109:21–22,26–27,30–31
Luke 13:31–35

NOVEMBER 1

Beloved: See what love the Father has bestowed on us that we
may be called the children of God.
—1 JOHN 3:1

On All Saints Day, I remember favorite saints, both
from history and from my own life. These vary from
year to year: at certain points in my life I have felt
drawn to such models as the avuncular pastoral style
of John XXIII, the inspired creativity of
St. Hildegard, or the warmth and devotion of my
grandmothers. I also consider my place in this "blest
communion, family divine" as the hymn "For All the
Saints" describes the communion of saints. God
wants me to find the special way to holiness. As
Thomas Merton writes, "For me to be a saint is to
be myself."

Revelation 7:2–4,9–14
Psalm 24:1bc–2,3–4ab,5–6
1 John 3:1–3
Matthew 5:1–12a

⇒ 335 ⇐

NOVEMBER 2

• THE COMMEMORATION OF ALL THE FAITHFUL DEPARTED
(ALL SOULS' DAY) •

*And this is the will of the one who sent me, that I should not
lose anything of what he gave me, but that I should raise it on
the last day.*
—JOHN 6:39

Someone I loved did something terrible and died not
long after. My casual belief in God's mercy was
tested as I truly feared for this person's soul. The
following All Souls' Day, I cried for him, as I had
most days since his death. A priest saw me after
Mass, and I confided why I was so upset. He asked,
"Do you love him?" When I nodded, he continued,
"Can you trust God to love him, too?"

Wisdom 3:1–9
Psalm 23:1–3a,3b–4,5,6
Romans 5:5–11 or 6:3–9
John 6:37–40
Other readings may be selected.

———————

Sunday

NOVEMBER 3

• THIRTY-FIRST SUNDAY IN ORDINARY TIME •

Before the LORD the whole universe is as a grain from
a balance
or a drop of morning dew come down upon the earth.
—WISDOM 11:22

The universe is like a drop of dew before the Lord.
We are even smaller molecules of that tiny droplet.
Yet God sees and values each of us individually and
loves each of us beyond measure.

Wisdom 11:22–12:2
Psalm 145:1–2,8–9,10–11,13,14
2 Thessalonians 1:11–2:2
Luke 19:1–10

Monday

NOVEMBER 4

• ST. CHARLES BORROMEO, BISHOP •

Oh, the depth of the riches and wisdom and knowledge of
God! How inscrutable are his judgments and how
unsearchable his ways!
—ROMANS 11:33

When I look over my life, I see so many unexpected,
unearned blessings, poured out of God's abundance.
I give thanks for the depths of divine goodness.

Romans 11:29–36
Psalm 69:30–31,33–34,36
Luke 14:12–14

⇒ 338 ⇐

> *"The servant went and reported this to his master. Then the master of the house in a rage commanded his servant, 'Go out quickly into the streets and alleys of the town and bring in here the poor and the crippled, the blind and the lame.'"*
> —LUKE 14:21

A dinner host is spurned by his guests in today's parable from Luke. He enjoins his servant to fill his table with the poor and needy, banishing any of the inviting guests from dining at his table. This parable has always given me pause: are God's feelings hurt when we don't reply to the invitation to dine in the kingdom? That's how I feel when people don't come to my parties. Maybe this is excessive anthropomorphizing, but I am convinced of one thing: the master wants a full house.

Romans 12:5–16b
Psalm 131:1bcde,2,3
Luke 14:15–24

NOVEMBER 6

*Love does no evil to the neighbor; hence, love is the fulfillment
of the law.*
—ROMANS 13:10

God wants us to love each other. This is challenging
and revolutionary. Imagine how different our world
would be if we better observed this commandment:
no violence, no bickering, no hunger, total peace.
Imagining this utopia is the easy part. Now imagine
how a life lived in perfect love might transform the
world closest to you: your family, friends, and
neighbors. How much of this transformation do we
have the ability to begin, here and now?

Romans 13:8–10
Psalm 112:1b–2,4–5,9
Luke 14:25–33

NOVEMBER 7

One thing I ask of the LORD;
this I seek:
To dwell in the house of the LORD
all the days of my life,
That I may gaze on the loveliness of the LORD
and contemplate his temple.
—PSALM 27:4

When I arrive home at the end of the day, I'm relieved. I know where things are. I'm surrounded by objects that remind me of those I love, and I can feel my family's presence in each room. I'm sheltered from the elements, and I have the tools to light up the dark. But even with all these comforts, I wonder how much more comforting God's house must be!

Romans 14:7–12
Psalm 27:1bcde,4,13–14
Luke 15:1–10

NOVEMBER 8

*I myself am convinced about you, my brothers and sisters,
that you yourselves are full of goodness, filled with all
knowledge, and able to admonish one another.*
—ROMANS 15:14

In today's reading, Paul writes a letter to the
Christian community in Rome in which he corrects
their behavior. At the same time, he notes that they
can be a healthy community on their own. Balancing
the desire or need to correct with respect for the
capability of people to correct themselves is an
ongoing act of adjustment. We can't abandon this
responsibility to correct because it is awkward;
healthy communities require healthy accountability.
As St. John XXIII advised, "See everything, overlook
a great deal, correct a little."

Romans 15:14–21
Psalm 98:1,2–3ab,3cd–4
Luke 16:1–8

NOVEMBER 9

*Do you not know that you are the temple of God, and that the
Spirit of God dwells in you?*
—1 CORINTHIANS 3:16

My relationship with my body has always been
fraught. I was unathletic as a child, unable to
accomplish much in gym class, and usually last in
races. My body was a disappointment, a conviction
that was confirmed when I developed a chronic
illness in adulthood. Every day I struggle to cherish
this body that can run, dance, sing, and
embrace—to cherish it for being the vehicle that lets
me live my blessed life.

Ezekiel 47:1–2,8–9,12
Psalm 46:2–3,5–6,8–9
1 Corinthians 3:9c–11,16–17
John 2:13–22

NOVEMBER 10

*But the Lord is faithful; he will strengthen you and guard you
from the evil one.*
—2 THESSALONIANS 3:3

The strength God gives to us is rarely superhero
strength—it's usually more human (and thus, more
attainable). Anne Lamott describes it like this in her
book *Traveling Mercies:* "I always imagined when I was
a kid that adults had some kind of inner toolbox, full
of shiny tools: the saw of discernment, the hammer
of wisdom, the sandpaper of patience. But then
when I grew up I found that life handed you these
rusty bent old tools—friendships, prayer,
conscience, honesty—and said, Do the best you can
with these, they will have to do. And mostly, against
all odds, they're enough."

2 Maccabees 7:1–2,9–14
Psalm 17:1,5–6,8,15 (15b)
2 Thessalonians 2:16—3:5
Luke 20:27–38 or 20:27,34–38

Monday

NOVEMBER 11

• ST. MARTIN OF TOURS, BISHOP •

And the Apostles said to the Lord, "Increase our faith."
—LUKE 17:5

Even though they had an up-close view of Jesus'
ministry, the apostles still felt their faith was lacking.
Can you seek out deepening faith while also being
content with the gifts of faith you have already
received?

Wisdom 1:1–7
Psalm 139:1b–3,4–6,7–8,9–10
Luke 17:1–6

• ST. JOSAPHAT, BISHOP AND MARTYR •

Those who trust in him shall understand truth,
and the faithful shall abide with him in love:
Because grace and mercy are with his holy ones,
and his care is with his elect.
—WISDOM 3:9

The promise to the just is not to receive riches or
accolades but to understand truth and to live forever
in the love, grace, and mercy of God.

Wisdom 2:23–3:9
Psalm 34:2–3,16–17,18–19
Luke 17:7–10

Defend the lowly and the fatherless;
render justice to the afflicted and the destitute.
Rescue the lowly and the poor;
from the hand of the wicked deliver them.
—PSALM 82:3–4

A dear friend often repeats the advice he got from a
mentor while finishing a postgraduate volunteer
program: stay close to the poor. The Scripture is
very clear about our responsibility to the poor,
vulnerable, and oppressed. Our proximity will breed
compassion and action.

Wisdom 6:1–11
Psalm 82:3–4,6–7
Luke 17:11–19

NOVEMBER 14

Asked by the Pharisees when the Kingdom of God would come, Jesus said in reply, "The coming of the Kingdom of God cannot be observed, and no one will announce, 'Look, here it is,' or, 'There it is.' For behold, the Kingdom of God is among you."
—LUKE 17:20–21

Most days, if I lift my head and look around, I see some type of obligation. There are papers to grade, songs to learn, e-mails to answer. I remind myself that these are my ways of engaging with the world. Each interaction with art, learning, or another person is a way that God is made known. Breathe deeply. Look around. The kingdom of God is among you.

Wisdom 7:22b–8:1
Psalm 119:89,90,91,130,135,175
Luke 17:20–25

"Whoever seeks to preserve his life will lose it, but whoever loses it will save it."

—LUKE 17:33

Is there a part of your life in which you are tempted to be stingy because you fear you won't have "enough"? What if you trusted that you could give away whatever you're holding back? Would this free you in some way?

Wisdom 13:1–9
Psalm 19:2–3,4–5ab
Luke 17:26–37

Glory in his holy name;
rejoice, O hearts that seek the LORD!
—PSALM 105:3

When I was quite young, I would ride the city bus
into downtown Hartford with my grandmother, who
was also named Margaret, for lunch at the G. Fox
building. Sometimes other relatives with the same
name would join us for what we called "Margaret
parties." All these decades later, my gratitude for
such love only grows deeper, and I am certain that
all the Saint Margarets continue to pray for me.

Wisdom 18:14–16,19:6–9
Psalm 105:2–3,36–37,42–43
Luke 18:1–8

NOVEMBER 17

• THIRTY-THIRD SUNDAY IN ORDINARY TIME •

We hear that some are conducting themselves among you in a
disorderly way, by not keeping busy but minding the
business of others.
—2 THESSALONIANS 3:11

There are countless rationalizations for why we
should mind others' business, but Paul (and,
elsewhere, Jesus) is pretty clear that we shouldn't.
Getting my own spiritual house in order is more
than enough to keep me busy, and it is also
something over which I have control.

Malachi 3:19–20a
Psalm 98:5–6,7–8,9
2 Thessalonians 3:7–12
Luke 21:5–19

• THE DEDICATION OF THE BASILICAS OF SS. PETER AND PAUL, APOSTLES *
ST. ROSE PHILIPPINE DUCHESNE, VIRGIN •

*Give me life, O Lord,
and I will do your commands.*
—PSALM 119:88

When I was very sick, I avoided bargaining with
God. I didn't want to make promises out of
desperation or pain, but I knew I would use my
energy well if my health was given back to me. At
one point, I prayed a novena to St. John XXIII,
culminating in a visit to his tomb in St. Peter's
Basilica. My prayer now is the same as it was then:
"Good Pope John, by your kind and loving
intercession may we be kept in physical health to
better serve and renew the world."

1 Maccabees 1:10–15,41–43,54–57,62–63 or
Acts 28:11–16,30–31
Psalm 119:53,61,134,150,155,158 or
98:1,2–3ab,3cd–4,5–6
Luke 18:35–43 or Matthew 14:22–33

NOVEMBER 19

*Now a man there named Zacchaeus, who was a chief tax
collector and also a wealthy man, was seeking to see who
Jesus was; but he could not see him because of the crowd, for
he was short in stature. So he ran ahead and climbed a
sycamore tree in order to see Jesus, who was about to
pass that way.*
—LUKE 19:2–4

Zacchaeus's occupation and wealth were both
obstacles on his road to discipleship, but he dealt
with the most immediate impediment: his height.
This made all the difference. Any step closer to Jesus
can be life-changing.

2 Maccabees 6:18–31
Psalm 3:2–3,4–5,6–7
Luke 19:1–10

"Then the other servant came and said, 'Sir, here is your gold coin; I kept it stored away in a handkerchief, for I was afraid of you, because you are a demanding man; you take up what you did not lay down and you harvest what you did not plant.'"

—LUKE 19:20–21

Use the gifts you are given. Don't let fear of error paralyze you. Be moved to action by the trust God has in you.

2 Maccabees 7:1,20–31
Psalm 17:1bcd,5–6,8b and 15
Luke 19:11–28

NOVEMBER 21

• THE PRESENTATION OF THE BLESSED VIRGIN MARY •

To the upright I will show the saving power of God.
—PSALM 50:23

Living in uprightness gives us eyes better able to see
God at work in the world. Keep training your heart
to perceive the goodness of the Lord.

1 Maccabees 2:15–29
Psalm 50:1b–2,5–6,14–15
Luke 19:41–44

NOVEMBER 22

• ST. CECILIA, VIRGIN AND MARTYR •

We praise your glorious name, O mighty God.
—1 CHRONICLES 29:13

St. Cecilia is often painted with organ pipes in her
hand. She was known for hearing heavenly music
when she was married, and she is now the patron
saint of music. St. Cecilia, help us to make the world
more beautiful, peaceful, and joyful with our songs
of praise.

1 Maccabees 4:36–37,52–59
1 Chronicles
29:10bcd,11abc,11d–12a,12bcd
Luke 19:45–48

NOVEMBER 23

• ST. CLEMENT I, POPE AND MARTYR • ST. COLUMBAN, ABBOT • BLESSED
MIGUEL AGUSTÍN PRO, PRIEST AND MARTYR •

*They can no longer die, for they are like angels; and they are
the children of God because they are the ones who will rise.*
—LUKE 20:36

Blessed Miguel Pro went to his death with prayer
and confidence, proclaiming "Viva Cristo Rey!" In
true imitation of Christ, he prayed for the firing
squad carrying out his martyrdom. We honor his
witness when we offer our own difficult prayers.

1 Maccabees 6:1–13
Psalm 9:2–3,4 and 6,16 and 19
Luke 20:27–40

NOVEMBER 24

*When all the elders of Israel came to David in Hebron, King
David made an agreement with them there before the LORD,
and they anointed him king of Israel.*
—2 SAMUEL 5:3

David stayed close to the Lord and was a holy king.
When he strayed from the path, his sin was glaring.
Many leaders make such mistakes. We have a leader
in Christ Jesus who cannot stray from the true
holiness he is. His reign is one of peace and love.

2 Samuel 5:1–3
Psalm 122:1–2,3–4,4–5
Colossians 1:12–20
Luke 23:35–43

*He said, "I tell you truly, this poor widow put in more than
all the rest; for those others have all made offerings from their
surplus wealth, but she, from her poverty, has offered her
whole livelihood."*
—LUKE 21:3–4

If we wait until we have "enough" to be generous, we
may never have enough. Acts of charity remind us
who we are and what we value. They are statements
of faith.

Daniel 1:1–6,8–20
Daniel 3:52,53,54,55,56
Luke 21:1–4

NOVEMBER 26

*"You heavens, bless the Lord,
praise and exalt him above all forever."*
—DANIEL 3:59

As Ordinary Time nears its end, many of our
readings invite us to consider the end of time. We
can also think of those things that will not end: the
glory of God and the divine love that has always
been showered upon us.

Daniel 2:31–45
Daniel 3:57,58,59,60,61
Luke 21:5–11

NOVEMBER 27

*Daniel answered the king: "You may keep your gifts, or give
your presents to someone else; but the writing I will read for
you, O king, and tell you what it means."*
—DANIEL 5:17

In today's reading, Daniel shares the message of God
not for wealth but for the sake of the message. As
someone who teaches religion for a living, I feel a bit
of an indictment in this passage: I share the message
for money (though surely not for money alone!). Are
there other motivators that taint our ministries?
Self-satisfaction, pride, superiority, or fear can all
creep into our efforts at evangelization. Pray to stay
focused on the gospel—that love of it may be what
motivates our words and actions.

Daniel 5:1–6,13–14,16–17,23–28
Daniel 3:62,63,64,65,66,67
Luke 21:12–19

"Let the earth bless the Lord,
praise and exalt him above all forever."
—DANIEL 3:74

I am most thankful for God's pervasive grace and the
people in my life who reveal that grace to me. What
and whom do you offer thanks for today?

Daniel 6:12–28
Daniel 3:68,69,70,71,72,73,74
Luke 21:20–28

Jesus told his disciples a parable. "Consider the fig tree and all the other trees."
—LUKE 21:29

The New England trees show signs of a long, cold winter approaching. This season fills me with desolation and grief. I heed the words of Dorothy Day, who died on this date in 1980: "We have all known the long loneliness and we have learned that the only solution is love and that love comes with community."

Daniel 7:2–14
Daniel 3:75,76,77,78,79,80,81
Luke 21:29–33

He called them, and immediately they left their boat and their father and followed him.
—MATTHEW 4:21–22

At sundown, the Church enters Advent, a season of waiting for Jesus to come. Listen for his call, however it may come during these hectic weeks. May we, like Andrew and the other fishermen, follow where he leads.

Romans 10:9–18
Psalm 19:8,9,10,11
Matthew 4:18–22

Sunday

DECEMBER 1

• FIRST SUNDAY OF ADVENT •

"So too, you also must be prepared, for at an hour you do not
expect, the Son of Man will come."
—MATTHEW 24:44

Every decision we make has the potential to prepare
us to meet Jesus, however he may come to us. If we
keep this in mind, eventually we develop the habit
of choosing those things that make us ready.

Isaiah 2:1–5
Psalm 122:1–2,3–4,4–5,6–7,8–9
Romans 13:11–14
Matthew 24:37–44

For over all, the LORD's glory will be shelter and protection:
shade from the parching heat of day,
refuge and cover from storm and rain.
—ISAIAH 4:6

I live in an urban area where the reality of homelessness is apparent. Before I moved to a city, the idea of "homelessness" was nebulous, a term thrown around so often that it made this tragedy sound unavoidable. But is it? If we truly find homelessness unavoidable in today's culture and environment, we need to change the culture. The ubiquity of poverty is not a call to complacency but to conversion. Shelter is a gift of God, and when we offer it to others we are doing God's work.

Isaiah 4:2–6
Psalm 122:1–2,3–4b,4cd–5,6–7,8–9
Matthew 8:5–11

DECEMBER 3

• ST. FRANCIS XAVIER, PRIEST •

Justice shall be the band around his waist,
and faithfulness a belt upon his hips.
—ISAIAH 11:5

God's love of justice is prominent throughout
Scripture. I pray for the wisdom to give justice
similar attention in my personal morality. Giving a
dollar to a panhandler is far easier than remaining
constantly on the lookout for ways to make life
easier and fairer for the poor and vulnerable. This
may mean welcoming people into my community
who make me uncomfortable or sacrificing some of
my money or privilege to help someone get a leg up.
I strive to look beyond these discouraging moments
of discomfort or sacrifice, because there is no
question that working for justice will make me more
like Christ.

Isaiah 11:1–10
Psalm 72:1–2,7–8,12–13,17
Luke 10:21–24

*The crowds were amazed when they saw the mute speaking,
the deformed made whole, the lame walking, and the blind able
to see, and they glorified the God of Israel.*

—MATTHEW 15:31

Jesus uses his power to make us well. Such healing
would be astonishing even as an afterthought. It is
all the more magnificent to know that our healing is
his priority. God cares for us.

Isaiah 25:6–10a
Psalm 23:1–3a,3b–4,5,6
Matthew 15:29–37

*"Everyone who listens to these words of mine and acts on them
will be like a wise man who built his house on rock."*
—MATTHEW 7:24

There is no one right way to live a Christian life. As
long as my life is rooted in the gospel, I don't worry
about people who disagree with my choices. Jesus
told us to build our houses on him and his words,
but he didn't tell us there was only one way to
decorate them.

Isaiah 26:1–6
Psalm 118:1 and
8–9,19–21,25–27a
Matthew 7:21,24–27

*On that day the deaf shall hear
the words of a book;
And out of gloom and darkness,
the eyes of the blind shall see.*
—ISAIAH 29:18

"Something's Coming" from *West Side Story* is one of my favorite nonliturgical songs for Advent. Tony sings that something's coming, something good, though he has no idea of all that will transpire in the subsequent hours. Anticipating meeting Maria, he waits in eagerness, the same eagerness that characterizes Advent. God might surprise you this season. "Could be, who knows?"

Isaiah 29:17–24
Psalm 27:1,4,13–14
Matthew 9:27–31

DECEMBER 7

"Cure the sick, raise the dead, cleanse lepers, drive out demons.
Without cost you have received; without cost you are to give."
—MATTHEW 10:8

A prayer attributed to St. Ignatius of Loyola asks that
we may learn "to give and not to count the cost . . .
to labor and not to ask for any reward, save that of
knowing that I do your will." The Savior tells us to
do as he did, without counting the cost.

Isaiah 30:19–21,23–26
Psalm 147:1–2,3–4,5–6
Matthew 9:35–10:1,5a,6–8

DECEMBER 8

Welcome one another, then, as Christ welcomed you, for the glory of God.
—ROMANS 15:7

In this season of hospitality, many of us put extra care into keeping our homes warm and welcoming. Let us do the same with our hearts, so that the busyness of the season doesn't cause us to shut out anyone in need of companionship.

Isaiah 11:1–10
Psalm 72:1–2,7–8,12–13,17
Romans 15:4–9
Matthew 3:1–12

Monday

DECEMBER 9

• THE IMMACULATE CONCEPTION OF THE BLESSED VIRGIN MARY (PATRONAL
FEASTDAY OF THE UNITED STATES OF AMERICA) •

*He answered, "I heard you in the garden; but I was afraid
because I was naked, so I hid myself."*
—GENESIS 3:10

Adam's sin led him to fear, proof that sin's corrosion
of our relationships may last much longer than the
duration of a sinful act. Although we can't undo our
sins, we can break free of some of their effects
through honest penance and reconciliation. As we
prepare ourselves to meet the Lord, let us also take a
close look at anything that holds us back from
greeting him.

Genesis 3:9–15,20
Psalm 98:1,2–3ab,3cd–4
Ephesians 1:3–6,11–12
Luke 1:26–38

⟾ 373 ⟽

DECEMBER 10

*Jesus said to his disciples: "What is your opinion? If a man
has a hundred sheep and one of them goes astray, will he not
leave the ninety-nine in the hills and go in search of
the stray?"*
—MATTHEW 18:12

If someone else needs and receives more care and
attention than I, it's human nature for me to be
jealous, especially if I feel that bad behavior or
mistakes are being rewarded. Instead, can I be happy
that I am safe and secure and have all I need? Can I
not begrudge others the care they need?

Isaiah 40:1–11
Psalm 96:1–2,3 and
10ac,11–12,13
Matthew 18:12–14

Wednesday

DECEMBER 11

• ST. DAMASUS I, POPE •

Do you not know
or have you not heard?
The LORD is the eternal God,
creator of the ends of the earth.
He does not faint nor grow weary,
and his knowledge is beyond scrutiny.
He gives strength to the fainting;
for the weak he makes vigor abound.
—ISAIAH 40:28–29

On busy, wearying days, you may feel like God is
asking a lot of you, and indeed the bar is high: to
stay awake, to pray always, to be like Christ. But
God gives us strength to strive for these things and
shapes our hearts to desire them more deeply.

Isaiah 40:25–31
Psalm 103:1–2,3–4,8 and 10
Matthew 11:28–30

DECEMBER 12

• OUR LADY OF GUADALUPE •

*Mary said, "Behold, I am the handmaid of the Lord. May it
be done to me according to your word." Then the angel
departed from her.*
—LUKE 1:38

The stories of angels and apparitions are written
down. We hear less about the quiet moments of
solitude and contemplation during which feelings of
abandonment may surface. Many saints knew such
moments and called on the memories of communion
with God to bring their attention back to that
inscrutable nearness.

Zechariah 2:14–17 or
Revelation 11:19a,12:1–6a,10ab
Judith 13:18bcde,19
Luke 1:26–38 or 1:39–47

DECEMBER 13

Your descendants would be like the sand,
and those born of your stock like its grains,
Their name never cut off
or blotted out from my presence.
—ISAIAH 48:19

My paternal grandfather's family came from the
Sicilian city of Siracusa, which is under the
patronage of St. Lucy. Every time I do any research
into that branch of our family tree, I find more
women named Lucy. I only knew one, my father's
Aunt Lucy, but I find inspiration in the knowledge
that I stand on the shoulders of those who bear the
name that means "light."

Isaiah 48:17–19
Psalm 1:1–2,3,4 and 6
Matthew 11:16–19

In those days,
like a fire there appeared the prophet Elijah
whose words were as a flaming furnace.
—SIRACH 48:1

History is dotted with prophets who remind us of
the deepest truths. St. John of the Cross gave us the
phrase "dark night" as well as the wisdom that our
dark nights are where the light of our longing and
the light of Christ meet. As a hymn from the Taizé
community sings, "Within our darkest night, you
kindle the fire that never dies away."

Sirach 48:1–4,9–11
Psalm 80:2ac and
3b,15–16,18–19
Matthew 17:9a,10–13

Sunday

DECEMBER 15

• THIRD SUNDAY OF ADVENT •

Do not complain, brothers and sisters, about one another, that you may not be judged. Behold, the Judge is standing before the gates.
—JAMES 5:9

I imagine, hope, and pray that, if called upon, I could do glorious things for God. But instead of calling me to grand action and sacrifice, I am called to follow the word of the Lord in the mundanity of today's Scripture verse: do not complain. In truth this is a heavy and challenging sacrifice, requiring ongoing conversion and attentiveness to grace. I cannot sit back and wait for the moment when I will be required to demonstrate heroic virtue. I must orient my entire life toward the everyday virtues: a positive attitude and speech that uplifts.

Isaiah 35:1–6a,10
Psalm 146:6–7,8–9,9–10
James 5:7–10
Matthew 11:2–11

Guide me in your truth and teach me,
for you are God my savior.
—PSALM 25:5

I have been fortunate to teach many students who
truly want to learn. They are curious, receptive, and
inquisitive. I hope they never lose those qualities,
and I recognize how much I can learn from them.

Numbers 24:2–7,15–17a
Psalm 25:4–5ab,6 and 7bc,8–9
Matthew 21:23–27

*Thus the total number of generations from Abraham to David
is fourteen generations; from David to the Babylonian exile,
fourteen generations; from the Babylonian exile to the Christ,
fourteen generations.*
—MATTHEW 1:17

The genealogy of Jesus is not a captivating read: a
canon of patriarchs and five notable women. What
untold stories of holiness lie behind these names that
connect Jesus through Joseph to Abraham?

Genesis 49:2,8–10
Psalm 72:1–2,3–4ab,7–8,17
Matthew 1:1–17

DECEMBER 18

*When Joseph awoke, he did as the angel of the Lord had
commanded him and took his wife into his home.*
—MATTHEW 1:24

An angel tells Joseph to take Mary into his home
and to name her son Jesus, and he responds with
quiet obedience. The angel also told him not to be
afraid. Was he able to follow this command as well?

Jeremiah 23:5–8
Psalm 72:1–2,12–13,18–19
Matthew 1:18–25

DECEMBER 19

But they had no child, because Elizabeth was barren and both were advanced in years.
—LUKE 1:7

God is always creating new life in unexpected and inexplicable ways. When my chronic illness was at its worst, I was extremely weak. I could rarely be active for longer than a few minutes. Pain and nausea clouded my mind and judgment. I wasted away, and half of my hair fell out. I should look back on this time as nothing more than a walk in the valley of the shadow of death, but instead I remember the love of my family and friends, the attentive care of the man who would soon be my husband, and the growing understanding of how Jesus' suffering and Resurrection brought life to the darkest places of human existence. I don't think pain such as mine is required for wisdom, and I would not wish it on anyone, but I believe that when such pain and evil strike us, God can still find ways to draw new life from suffering.

Judges 13:2–7,24–25a
Psalm 71:3–4a,5–6ab,16–17
Luke 1:5–25

Friday

DECEMBER 20

*In the sixth month, the angel Gabriel was sent from God to a
town of Galilee called Nazareth, to a virgin betrothed to a
man named Joseph, of the house of David, and the virgin's
name was Mary.*
—LUKE 1:26–27

The Annunciation is retold frequently throughout
the liturgical calendar. Is it because this divine
encounter so transformed history? Because we need
reminders of the incredible truth that God became
human? Or because we need a reminder of the
equally incredible truth that Mary said *yes*?

Isaiah 7:10–14
Psalm 24:1–2,3–4ab,5–6
Luke 1:26–38

Saturday

DECEMBER 21

Our soul waits for the LORD,
who is our help and our shield,
For in him our hearts rejoice;
in his holy name we trust.
—PSALM 33:20–21

The days are cold and busy while I wait for the joy of the world. I wait attentively not out of fear but because I know Christ's love is the highest good. I pray with St. Peter Canisius: "Let my eyes take their sleep, but may my heart always keep watch for you."

Song of Songs 2:8–14 or
Zephaniah 3:14–18a
Psalm 33:2–3,11–12,20–21
Luke 1:39–45

*The LORD spoke to Ahaz, saying: Ask for a sign from the
LORD your God; let it be deep as the netherworld, or
high as the sky!*
—ISAIAH 7:10–11

For many years, I held back on acknowledging the
things for which I longed, believing that I didn't
deserve them. I couldn't ask God to guide me toward
my brightest future because I was scared to ask for
what I desired. There was no virtue in keeping
secrets from the One whose plan is illuminated and
revealed in our deepest desires. Let us offer up our
longings in prayer and ask to be guided by them
to holiness.

Isaiah 7:10–14
Psalm 24:1–2,3–4,5–6 (7c and 10b)
Romans 1:1–7
Matthew 1:18–24

DECEMBER 23

• ST. JOHN OF KANTY, PRIEST •

But who will endure the day of his coming?
And who can stand when he appears?
For he is like a refiner's fire,
or like the fuller's lye.
—MALACHI 3:2

The nearness of God can be terrifying when it reveals the distance between who we are and who we are called to be. But in the light of that fire, we see who we ought to be: shining children of the light.

Malachi 3:1–4,23–24
Psalm 25:4–5ab,8–9,10 and 14
Luke 1:57–66

DECEMBER 24

Forever I will maintain my kindness toward him,
and my covenant with him stands firm.
—PSALM 89:29

With the solstice just behind us and a new year
about to begin, time and transition may be on your
mind. Meditate these days on that which is timeless:
the bold, divine promise of forever.

2 Samuel 7:1–5,8b–12,14a,16
Psalm 89:2–3,4–5,27 and 29
Luke 1:67–79

Wednesday

DECEMBER 25

• THE NATIVITY OF THE LORD (CHRISTMAS) •

*But to those who did accept him he gave power to become
children of God, to those who believe in his name, who were
born not by natural generation nor by human choice nor by a
man's decision but of God.*

—JOHN 1:12–13

Ideally, Christmas Day is when my worldly
preparations of music, food, gifts, and cheer all come
to fruition. And it is all God's grace.

VIGIL:
Isaiah 62:1–5
Psalm 89:4–5,16–17,27,29 (2a)
Acts 13:16–17,22–25
Matthew 1:1–25 or 1:18–25

NIGHT:
Isaiah 9:1–6
Psalm 96:1–2,2–3,11–12,13
Titus 2:11–14
Luke 2:1–14

DAWN:
Isaiah 62:11–12
Psalm 97:1,6,11–12
Titus 3:4–7
Luke 2:15–20

DAY:
Isaiah 52:7–10
Psalm 98:1,2–3,3–4,5–6 (3c)
Hebrews 1:1–6
John 1:1–18 or 1:1–5,9–14

Thursday

DECEMBER 26

• ST. STEPHEN, THE FIRST MARTYR •

*For it will not be you who speak but the Spirit of your Father
speaking through you.*
—MATTHEW 10:20

When my efforts are focused more on burnishing my
image than on letting God work through me, I sell
myself short and miss out on being part of God's
mission.

Acts 6:8–10,7:54–59
Psalm 31:3cd–4,6 and 8ab,16bc and 17
Matthew 10:17–22

⇒ 390 ⇐

Friday

DECEMBER 27

• ST. JOHN, APOSTLE AND EVANGELIST •

Light dawns for the just,
and gladness, for the upright of heart.
—PSALM 97:11

John the Evangelist is the odd man out, having
written the Gospel that doesn't match the other
three. Matthew, Mark, and Luke, who include many
of the same stories, told using similar language, are
referred to as the "synoptic" Gospels, which literally
means "seeing together." John's different perspective
leaves us with a distinct testimony of Jesus' love,
enriching our faith. Let us listen to the unique voices
in our midst.

1 John 1:1–4
Psalm 97:1–2,5–6,11–12
John 20:1a,2–8

DECEMBER 28

• THE HOLY INNOCENTS, MARTYRS •

*Beloved: This is the message that we have heard from Jesus
Christ and proclaim to you: God is light, and in him there is
no darkness at all.*

—1 JOHN 1:5

In times of darkness, call on the memory of light. Let
your longing for it remind you of the ultimate
triumph of the God of light.

1 John 1:5–2:2
Psalm 124:2–3,4–5,7b–8
Matthew 2:13–18

⇒ 392 ⇐

DECEMBER 29

• THE HOLY FAMILY OF JESUS, MARY, AND JOSEPH •

Let the word of Christ dwell in you richly, as in all wisdom
you teach and admonish one another, singing psalms, hymns,
and spiritual songs with gratitude in your hearts to God.
—COLOSSIANS 3:16

If the Feast of the Holy Family reminds you of the
ways your family has let you down, think all the
more of the many families in your life to whom you
are connected by affection, if not by blood.
Remember the communities with whom you share
music, discussion, and gratitude, just as the
community in Colossae did thousands of years ago.
God bless all families.

Sirach 3:2–6,12–14
Psalm 128:1–2,3,4–5
Colossians 3:12–21 or 3:12–17
Matthew 2:13–15,19–23

*For all that is in the world, sensual lust, enticement for the
eyes, and a pretentious life, is not from the Father but is from
the world. Yet the world and its enticement are passing away.
But whoever does the will of God remains forever.*

—1 JOHN 2:16–17

God wants more for us than comfort, pleasure, and
superficial beauty. Those may be attractive but will
not truly satisfy. Seek what will endure forever.

1 John 2:12–17
Psalm 96:7–8a,8b–9,10
Luke 2:36–40

DECEMBER 31

• ST. SYLVESTER I, POPE •

All things came to be through him,
and without him nothing came to be.
—JOHN 1:3

As I say goodbye to the year, I look forward, not
back. I look toward the One who makes all things
and makes all things new. I set my eyes on the
goodness that is to come and how I can bring it
about, crying out as Alfred, Lord Tennyson did in "In
Memoriam": "Ring out old shapes of foul disease; /
Ring out the narrowing lust of gold; / Ring out the
thousand wars of old, / Ring in the thousand years
of peace."

1 John 2:18–21
Psalm 96:1–2,11–12,13
John 1:1–18

ABOUT THE AUTHOR

Margaret Felice is an educator, writer, and musician. She teaches religion and music at Boston College High School, and her writing on spirituality and the arts has been published in numerous magazines and online journals. Trained as a classical singer, she is an active performer and music minister. She lives in Boston with her husband, journalist Robert Goulston.

Silhouette®

COMING NEXT MONTH

Available September 28, 2010

SPECIAL EDITION

REQUEST YOUR FREE BOOKS!
2 FREE NOVELS PLUS 2 FREE GIFTS!

SPECIAL EDITION
Life, Love and Family!

YES! Please send me 2 FREE Silhouette® Special Edition® novels and my 2 FREE gifts (gifts are worth about $10). After receiving them, if I don't wish to receive any more books, I can return the shipping statement marked "cancel." If I don't cancel, I will receive 6 brand-new novels every month and be billed just $4.24 per book in the U.S. or $4.99 per book in Canada. That's a saving of 15% off the cover price! It's quite a bargain! Shipping and handling is just 50¢ per book.* I understand that accepting the 2 free books and gifts places me under no obligation to buy anything. I can always return a shipment and cancel at any time. Even if I never buy another book from Silhouette, the two free books and gifts are mine to keep forever.

235/335 SDN E5RG

Name	(PLEASE PRINT)	
Address		Apt. #
City	State/Prov.	Zip/Postal Code

Signature (if under 18, a parent or guardian must sign)

Mail to the Silhouette Reader Service:
IN U.S.A.: P.O. Box 1867, Buffalo, NY 14240-1867
IN CANADA: P.O. Box 609, Fort Erie, Ontario L2A 5X3

Not valid for current subscribers to Silhouette Special Edition books.

Want to try two free books from another line?
Call 1-800-873-8635 or visit www.morefreebooks.com.

* Terms and prices subject to change without notice. Prices do not include applicable taxes. N.Y. residents add applicable sales tax. Canadian residents will be charged applicable provincial taxes and GST. Offer not valid in Quebec. This offer is limited to one order per household. All orders subject to approval. Credit or debit balances in a customer's account(s) may be offset by any other outstanding balance owed by or to the customer. Please allow 4 to 6 weeks for delivery. Offer available while quantities last.

Your Privacy: Silhouette is committed to protecting your privacy. Our Privacy Policy is available online at www.eHarlequin.com or upon request from the Reader Service. From time to time we make our lists of customers available to reputable third parties who may have a product or service of interest to you. If you would prefer we not share your name and address, please check here. ☐

Help us get it right—We strive for accurate, respectful and relevant communications. To clarify or modify your communication preferences, visit us at www.ReaderService.com/consumerschoice.

SSE10R

HARLEQUIN®

A Romance

FOR EVERY MOOD™

Spotlight on

Inspirational

Wholesome romances
that touch the heart and soul.

See the next page
to enjoy a sneak peek from
the Love Inspired® inspirational series.

*See below for a sneak peek at
our inspirational line, Love Inspired®.
Introducing HIS HOLIDAY BRIDE
by bestselling author Jillian Hart*

Autumn Granger gave her horse rein to slide toward the town's new sheriff.

"Hey, there." The man in a brand-new Stetson, black T-shirt, jeans and riding boots held up a hand in greeting. He stepped away from his four-wheel drive with "Sheriff" in black on the doors and waded through the grasses. "I'm new around here."

"I'm Autumn Granger."

"Nice to meet you, Miss Granger. I'm Ford Sherman, from Chicago." He knuckled back his hat, revealing the most handsome face she'd ever seen. Big blue eyes contrasted with his sun-tanned complexion.

"I'm guessing you haven't seen much open land. Out here, you've got to keep an eye on cows or they're going to tear your vehicle apart."

"What?" He whipped around. Sure enough, mammoth black-and-white creatures had started to gnaw on his four-wheel drive. They clustered like a mob, mouths and tongues and teeth bent on destruction. One cow tried to pry the wiper off the windshield, another chewed on the side mirror. Several leaned through the open window, licking the seats.

"Move along, little dogie." He didn't know the first thing about cattle.

The entire herd swiveled their heads to study him curiously. Not a single hoof shifted. The animals soon returned to chewing, licking, digging through his possessions.

Autumn laughed, a warm and wonderful sound. "Thanks,

I needed that." She then pulled a bag from behind her saddle and waved it at the cows. "Look what I have, guys. Cookies."

Cows swung in her direction, and dozens of liquid brown eyes brightened with cookie hopes. As she circled the car, the cattle bounded after her. The earth shook with the force of their powerful hooves.

"Next time, you're on your own, city boy." She tipped her hat. The cowgirl stayed on his mind, the sweetest thing he had ever seen.

Will Ford be able to stick it out in the country
to find out more about Autumn?
Find out in HIS HOLIDAY BRIDE
by bestselling author Jillian Hart,
available in October 2010
only from Love Inspired®.

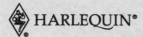
HARLEQUIN®

American ★ Romance®

Babies & Bachelors USA

Texas Legacies: The McCabes

The McCabes of Texas are back!
5 new stories from popular author

CATHY GILLEN THACKER

The Triplets' First Thanksgiving
(October 2010)

Paige Chamberlain desperately wants to be a mother…
but helping former rival Kurt McCabe raise three
abandoned babies isn't quite what she had in mind.
There's going to be a full house at the McCabe
residence this holiday season!

Also watch for
A Cowboy under the Mistletoe *(December 2010)*

"LOVE, HOME & HAPPINESS"

www.eHarlequin.com

HAR75329